5

Dear

It's a pleasure cruising through life together on the Island Princess. I hope this little book will help make your journey through life.

God has a message in here written to you

Enjoy
Jim

Please show this

A Rose Garden:
Living in Concert with Spirit

James J. Brown

Awaken Publishing
A division of 2211 Company, LLC
Seattle, WA, USA

A Rose Garden:
Living in Concert with Spirit
James J. Brown

Published by
Awaken Publishing
A division of 2211 Company, LLC
PO Box 25648
Seattle, WA 98165-1148
Awakenpublishing.net

All rights reserved. No part of this book may be reproduced or transmitted in any form or by any means, electronic or mechanical, including photocopying, recording or by any information storage and retrieval system without written permission from the author, except for the inclusion of brief quotations in a review.

© 2005 James J. Brown. All rights reserved.
Published 2005
Printed in the United States of America

Cover art by Melinda Thayne

ISBN 0-9729259-3-7: $13.95

Printed in The United State of America

To my beautiful wife, Rosemarie.
Without your love and support, this book would have been impossible.

"Life is a language in which certain truths are conveyed to us; if we could learn them in some other way, we should not live."
Arthur Schopenhauer

Contents

Part 1

Navigating the Rose Garden Called Your Life	2
Life Isn't Fair	5
You Made Your Life's Blueprint Before You Came Here	8
There Are No Victims!	10
You Are A Spiritual Being	13
There's Enough to Go Around	15
You Always Do the Best You Can With the Resources You Have Available	18
You Are Not the General Manager of the World	21
Whatever You Resist Persists	24
Your Past Doesn't Have to Determine Your Present	27
We Are All in Life Together	30
Everyone is a Winner	33
You Will Die	34

Part 2

Life Is a Perception	38
You Are the Only Person Who Sees Life the Way You Do	40
Have an Attitude of Gratitude!	43
Accept Responsibility for Everything That Happens to You	46
Focus on the Important Things	48
Be All That You Can Be	50
Take Life One Step at a Time	53
It's Not What Happens to You That Matters, It's What You Do About It	55
Ease and Dis-Ease	58
Would You Rather Be Right or Happy?	60
Be Flexible	62
Your Parents Couldn't Teach You Skills They Didn't Have	64
Leave a Lasting Legacy	66

Part 3

You Co-Create Your Universe	70
The Power of Thoughts	72
Life Will Change	74
To Change the Outcomes in Your Life, You Must Change Your Actions	76
Reprogram Your Subconscious Mind	78
Abundance	80
The Importance of Values	82
Honor the Beauty and the Differences in Others	84
Communication	86
Learn the Art of Listening	89
Learn to Manage the Energies of Life	91
The Cost of Holding a Grudge	94
Happiness Is a State of Mind	97

Part 4

You Will Learn Lessons	100
A Lesson Is Repeated Until it Is Learned	102
There Are No Mistakes—Only Lessons	104
Life's Greatest Periods of Growth Usually Follow Life's Tragedies	106
Others Are Mirrors of You	109
What You Make of Your Life Is up to You	112
Keep It Simple	114
See Life Through Rose-Colored Glasses	116
Life Is Never What It Seems to Be	118
Accept Yourself and Others Just As You Are	120
Don't Judge	122
The Answers Lie Within You	124
Your Power Lies Within You	126

Part 5

Love Yourself	130
Forgive Yourself and Others	133
Believe in Yourself	136
Be True to Yourself	138

Always Hope	141
Nobody Can Hurt Your Feelings Without Your Permission	144
You Have Exactly What You Believe You Deserve in Life	146
There Is Another Way to Look at This	149
Have Faith in Yourself and Others	152
What I Love About Myself	155
The Value of Wisdom	157
Live Life One Hundred Percent	159
It's the Quality of the Years You Live That Matters Not the Quantity	162

Part 6

The Golden Rule	166
You're Never Alone	169
Treat Your Body as a Sacred Temple	171
Your Most Important Relationship Is the One With Yourself	173
The Power of Prayer	176
Give Love	178
Let Go, Let God	180
Trust Your Creator	182
Someday You Will Understand	184
Ask Better Questions	186
There is a Silver Lining in Every Cloud	187
There is More to Life Than What We Experience With Our Five Senses	190
Life is Sacred	192
Appendix	194

Preface

The title "A Rose Garden: Living in Concert with Spirit" came to me during a walk. I had been thinking about writing a book for years and had come up with many different titles, none of which felt right. That is, none of them made me believe I was expert enough to write on the topic. But this title really felt good.

I wanted to write a collection of essays on a variety of topics that most of us deal with in our lives. I started writing down all the ideas that came to me. My fear was that there wouldn't be enough topics. That had always been my fear in my thirteen years of pubic speaking—that I wouldn't have enough material to cover the allotted time. But it never happened once. In fact, I seldom covered all the material I had planned. The same thing happened here; the topics kept multiplying. I liked them all, but we did cut some with the intention of making this book more meaningful for your life.

I started by working on the computer but found that I was constantly distracted by errors. I started dictating and was amazed at what came out of my mouth. I truly believe that it came from a higher source. At the end of many of these essays, "Amen" seemed to be the only logical thing I could say.

How you use the book is up to you. I will use it as a reference to go to when I need courage, strength hope or guidance to deal with an experience I am having. My hope is that it will stay with you for the rest of your life, because you are constantly changing and growing, and what didn't have meaning to you when you read it the first time may have meaning in your life ten or twenty years from now.

Acknowledgements

I would like to thank the following people for their great literary works and tremendous influence on me and the content of this book: Anthony Robbins; Louise Hay; Silvia Browne; Wayne Dyer, Ph.D.; Jerry Jampolsky, M.D.; Joseph Murphy; Robert Fulghum; Drunvalo Melchizedek; Deepak Chopra, M.D.; Steven Covey, Ph.D.; Julia Cameron; Ernest Holmes; Og Mandino; Dan Millman; James Redfield; Marianne Williamson; Neal Donald Walsh; Carolyn Miller, Ph.D.; James Van Praagh; Helen Schucman and William Thetford (*The Course in Miracles*); Eugene Whitworth; Shakti Gawain; and Gary Zukav.

This book owes its life to my wife Rosemarie who lets me do my thing. Thanks to Lynette Butcher who convinced me to take this out of moth balls and get it edited; that gave me the confidence that I am a writer. Thanks to our two sons Mike and Matt—Mike for being one of my life's greatest teachers, and Matt for having the maturity to transition from my being "pa" to being best friends.

On a personal note, thanks to Rijckie Colberg for her love, support and guidance over the last thirteen years. To Gina Como for her great sense of humor and friendship. To Lola Gillebaard for giving me confidence when I started speaking and telling me what a keynote was—after I had booked five of them without knowing what they were! To Ravi Chakko for being my first male friend as an adult. To Chuck Lacy, for your love and support, for always being there, for your generosity, and for seeing and loving me and not judging me by society's standards. That's a gift I will cherish the rest of my life.

I am thankful for the support of my speakers group, The Gold Coast group, especially Dan Poynter and Jim Zinger.

Thanks to Rossie Kichik for coming to ten of my cruise ship talks and staying in touch ever since via e-mail. To Paul Kovelman for working out with me for the last nine years and listening to me ramble on. To Rev. Carrie Lauer for being my spiritual guide through the challenges that arose during the writing of this book.

Thanks to my wife's cousin Maryanne Mills for all the long philosophical discussions over the last thirty-seven years and for thinking of me as her favorite philosopher. To Joe Pirrello for being a friend from the day we met at his wedding. We've had fun watching each other grow and pursue our life paths. To Mike Rounds for always being there to help in any way he could.

Thanks to everybody in my Alchemist 3 class who loved me and helped me open my heart. Thanks to Linda Barker who got me started on this leg of my spiritual growth. Thanks to the greatest influence on my spiritual life today, Holly Draper. Your insight, guidance, wisdom and love have resulted in my finding the lost treasures of my life. For this and you I am eternally grateful. In honor to you I will do everything I can to help others find their true beauty and their path.

Introduction

This book is written for people who are searching for a higher meaning to the events of their lives. Every day, we have hundreds of experiences, most of them inconsequential. But all of us have had things happen in our lives that completely changed our paths.

We go through most of our lives unconsciously, developing hundreds of habits so that we don't have to think about doing repetitive tasks. For example, I'll bet that you take a shower the same way and in the same sequence every time. As an experiment, next time you take a shower, put the soap in the other hand and start at the other end of your body. Count how many times you drop the bar of soap. It forces you to think about something you aren't used to thinking about. This holds true for just about everything we do. Consequently, when something big happens, we often don't stop to think about its purpose.

I am inviting you to adapt the point of view that everything that happens in your life is there to teach you a lesson! If your belief is that things just happen randomly, then this book isn't for you. But if we believe that things happen for a reason, then we want to find that reason and discover how we can benefit from every event. We do that by looking at the beliefs we have adopted in our lives and deciding that some of them no longer have value.

We all want the highest quality of life possible. Everyone will have problems in his or her life. The key is how we handle the problems and how we grow from them. The purpose of this book is to give you tools to evaluate areas of your life that aren't working to your satisfaction as well as steps for overcoming problems. If you assume that everything that happens to you is there to teach you a lesson, the question you must ask yourself is, "What is this here to teach me?" This will take your mind in a whole new direction. The key is to be open to the possibilities!

I have been talking to audiences all over the world about personal change for more than thirteen years, and I know that we are creatures of habit. I know that no one will go through all of these essays and do all of the exercises and completely transform their lives. Nevertheless, as you read this book, listen when your heart speaks to you. When you get to a key issue, your heart will tug at you, indicating that this is an area you are ready to change. My suggestion is to start with the area in which you believe you have the highest probability of achieving success. That will give you the motivation to try another. Set a goal for yourself and reward yourself for achieving it. Then go to the next one. Do it at your pace, not my pace. This is like a buffet dinner: You're free to pick and choose.

The intent of this book is to discuss specific thoughts, attitudes, and beliefs, and to provide exercises to help you deal with a particular topic. Each chapter will end with an affirmation. My spiritual teacher, Holly Draper, says take what fits and shelve the rest. This is your life, and only you should be deciding what works in your life, what doesn't work, and what you are ready to change.

As you journey through this book, remember that you came to this life as perfect love. Many things happened to strip this love of its rightful place on the gorgeous pedestal of your life. Some of the essays will discuss these events and some of them will discuss what you need to do to restore the luster to your pedestal and to place your perfect love back on its rightful throne.

I also encourage you to hang on to this book. If you read it with a specific objective in mind, I believe you will get a lot more out of it. Pick it up again in a year or two and read it again. You will be in a different place then, and something different will speak to you. If you want to share this book, buy a copy and give it to a friend or relative.

This is your life, and you are entitled to live it at the highest level. Life is a process, not an event. Make the most out of your journey. You are entitled to the maximum benefit possible. Above all, know that you are an incredible being, who has a tremendous amount of talent to contribute to the quality of life on this planet. Be bold, be brave, reach out and do what you have to do to function at the highest level.

I remember John F. Kennedy saying in 1961 that before the end of that decade we would put a man on the moon. Everyone thought he was crazy. That was impossible! But we, in fact, did go to the moon by 1968. Congratulations on having the courage to explore your life, and have a fabulous journey to within yourself, where all your answers reside. Now I wish you all the best as you begin your own incredible journey.

Disclaimer

This book is designed to help the reader search for the answers to the questions raised by life's experiences. The author is not a professional psychologist or counselor and is not engaged in rendering professional counseling services. If professional counseling is required, the services of a competent professional should be sought.

Part 1

Facts About How Life Works

A Rose Garden

Navigating the Rose Garden Called Your Life

"The world is a rose; smell it and pass it to your friends."
Persian Proverb

Our lives are filled with beautiful roses, and sometimes thorns and weeds. What will determine whether you focus on the beautiful rose blooms, the rosebuds, the dead roses, the thorns or the weeds? My perception is that it is our thoughts, attitudes, and beliefs that determine what we focus on in our life. Thoughts, attitudes, and beliefs—these are the three things that will help you protect the roses in your garden of experience.

It is widely held that we think 60,000 thoughts a day. There's only one person who thinks the thoughts in your brain—it's you. Therefore, it should be fairly easy for us to accept that we are responsible for the thoughts we think. The problem is that 80% to 95% of these thoughts are negative. Knowing this, it is important that we hire a gatekeeper of sorts, whose job is to decide which thoughts stay and which ones must leave.

However, our gatekeeper is always sleeping and all of our thoughts, especially the toxic negative ones, get in. Once they are in our brains they wreak havoc! They poison our life by getting us to be fearful, cynical, skeptical, limited, angry, hostile, violent, abusive, negligent, stuck, intolerant, judgmental, greedy, thievish, selfish, belligerent, and the list goes on. It's easy to understand why our lives seem to be in a constant state of upheaval, chaos, filled with problems, and stressful. It's funny—we'd never invite somebody into our home, whose shoes are filled with mud and who is dripping water from head to toe. We'd never let them walk all over our house, sit on our couch and generally make a mess of our home. Yet we allow these destructive toxic thoughts trample all over our brain and emotions, literally destroying our lives. We act as if they aren't even there.

The key to filtering out a negative thought is to make a decision: if this thought is allowed to stay, will it contribute to your living your life at the highest level possible? If not, kick it out! And every time it returns—and it will too, until it is absolutely certain it will never be welcome in your brain—say: "you are not welcome in my life now or ever! Leave immediately and never return."

The thoughts that you allowed to stay in the past were like seeds planted in your brain, and all of them grew up to become beliefs. Some of these beliefs served you well to get through a particularly difficult phase of your life. Say for example that as a child you were abused by a male. Through that experience, you developed the belief that you couldn't trust males. This belief got you through that trauma, but now it's twenty years later. As an adult, you still carry the belief that men can't be trusted, and that's had a big impact on your relationships. It's time to ask yourself if this belief serves you in your life today. If not, you can destroy it, and replace it with a belief that will serve you in your life today.

These beliefs generate your attitude about every situation. Negative thoughts create negative beliefs and negative beliefs generate negative attitudes. Never will a negative thought create a positive belief! And never will a negative belief generate a positive attitude. The key is awareness. Recognize a negative attitude, and ask two questions: What's my belief about this? What do I have to believe about this in order to have a positive attitude about it?

Often, we are not ready to change, and we choose to stay stuck. Remember, the only reason we do anything is that there is a payoff.

A Rose Garden

Ask yourself, what is my payoff in staying stuck? Often, there will be a negative payoff, but that's alright. Sometimes we stay stuck because we believe that if we change, this change will threaten our identity as a human being. Our perception is that all of our self-worth is wrapped up in our identity.

Exercise:

Hopefully, you are asking yourself, how do I find out what my beliefs are? Here is a partial list of categories which may help you begin to look at your own views. For each item on the list ask: What's my belief about this? Some of you may want to know where this belief came from. My point of view is it doesn't matter, but if it's important to you, ask yourself where the belief comes from, and write down the first thought that occurs to you.

My looks	Big business
My health	Politics
My emotions	Government
My age	Gays
My ability to learn	Lesbians
My children	My inner peace

Jot down the belief. Then ask if it still serves you. If not, create a belief that serves you today. This is your life, and it is your birthright to have beliefs that serve you today. Review the beliefs that are causing the most damage to your life today. Take as much time as you need. Do it in several sessions if that's more comfortable for you. Make it like a spring cleaning. You deserve to clean out old beliefs that no longer serve you, at least once a year.

Affirmation:

My life is filled with bouquets of gorgeous roses in full-bloom.

Life Isn't Fair

"Nothing in life is to be feared. It is only to be understood."
Marie Curry

Most of us would probably admit that life isn't fair. The problem, however, isn't in that belief but in how we respond to the bad things that happen in life. We may think we understand the fact that life isn't fair, yet when something happens that we don't consider to be fair, we often get upset.

I have been speaking in the healthcare industry for thirteen years, and have enjoyed it very much. But because of changes in that industry, it has become very difficult for me to get companies to sponsor my speaking engagements. The message I'm receiving is that it's time for me to do other things, such as speak on other topics or write. However, I am very reluctant to make these changes, because I love speaking about healthcare so much and am extremely comfortable with those audiences. Therefore, deep down, my belief is that life isn't being fair to me. I should be allowed to continue to do what I love so much, in the arena where I have earned respect and gained knowledge. On one hand, I say I understand that life isn't fair, but on the other hand, when something unfair happens to me, I get upset.

This chapter will help you bridge the gap between what you know on an intellectual basis and how you react to life situations. The first thing you need to do is consciously recognize when you're upset about an unfortunate circumstance. You may ask yourself, "Is this fair?" Of course, the answer is no. That is where you have the opportunity to change your response from an emotional one to one that is for your ultimate good. The question to ask instead is, "What lesson can I learn

A Rose Garden

here?"

I have had to realize that I am a good speaker, but it may be time for me to speak in arenas other than the healthcare industry. I'm also here to learn how to write and to communicate through the written word in addition to the spoken word. I am being challenged to grow beyond my current comfort zone. This is about what I will learn about myself during the process.

Can you see how this thought process would apply to a situation that you may be dealing with? When you allow your emotional reactions to control your life, you're going to be frustrated, and you're going to stay stuck. We cannot allow our fears to control our lives! In her book *Feel the Fear and Do It Anyway*, Susan Jeffers wrote that the only way out of fear is to go through it. The more we challenge our fears, the less control they will have over our lives! Therefore, when we have the courage to challenge our fears, our reward will be living a life at its highest level, with complete and total fulfillment. With that as our goal, let us begin the process of learning what we need to know.

Exercise:

Write down the most unfair thing that has happened in your life. Make a list of all the things you learned from that experience. How are you different? How are you a better person? How are you more mature? How are you a wiser person? Remember that life is a never-ending school. It will continue to teach you lessons. Some of them are easy and fun; some are extremely painful. You are here to learn! Practice being grateful for those lessons. You will either learn them from unfair situations, or life will present you more! Either way, you will learn.

Affirmation:

Everything that happens to me—past, present and future—is gently planned by one whose only purpose is my good. (Paraphrased from *A Course in Miracles*, Workbook, p. 247 1st edition p 255 2nd edition)

A Rose Garden

You Made Your Life's Blueprint Before You Came Here

"Before we leave The Other Side for our lifetime on earth, we compose an incredibly detailed chart of every aspect of our upcoming incarnation." Silvia Browne

Your life is unfolding according to plan. If this sounds like a new concept, I'm asking you to suspend your judgment about life—what it's about and how it happens. I'm asking you to be flexible and open to embracing the concept that you created a life plan for yourself before you were ever born, and that the purpose of that plan is to accomplish what you want in this life.

I believe this, and the belief has changed my own life. In her book *Blessings from the Other Side,* Sylvia Browne says that "we compose these charts [plans] on the other side, after we've made the choice to experience another life on Earth, which means that free will is an essential part of the process from the very beginning." She talks about how the details in our charts—every tiny aspect of our lives—are all specifically chosen based on what we've already experienced in past lives, our interim time on the other side and what we determine to accomplish in this life.

Once we've set our objectives, we come into our lives and begin the process of experiencing these lessons. We have choice and free will, and in that choice and free will, we can decide if we want these lessons to be easy or difficult. You may have chosen to learn your lessons the hard way. At any time in your life, you can choose to learn the easy way.

After we've made our blueprint and come into this life, we forget the lessons that we've come here to learn. The reason we forget is that if we had foreknowledge of our lives, we probably wouldn't put ourselves in the circumstances that enable us to learn lessons. For example, a neighbor of mine, Doug, went rock climbing the day after Christmas in 1989 and fell eighty-seven feet, landing on the base of his neck. He was left a quadriplegic. Doctors performed surgery to restore movement to his upper body. Had Doug known that he was going to fall that day, he never would have gone rock climbing. However, because he was on a path of destruction with drugs at the time that he fell, today, he says that the only reason that he is alive is because he did fall. It took that experience to catapult him through an important lesson about the sacredness of life.

Or perhaps you have experienced a divorce. You probably wouldn't have gotten married if you had known you were going to get divorced and that it was going to be painful. Maybe you have lost a child and think that if you had known the baby was going to die, you never would have had it. The important thing in these circumstances is to accept that we create and bring to us the events of our lives so that we might fulfill our life plans.

Exercise:

In what area of your life have you experienced the greatest growth? Identify some of the major events in your life that contributed to that growth, whether it was a tremendous victory or painful defeat. What did you learn from those events? How do you think these events contributed to your perception of life?

Affirmation:

I live my life on purpose.

A Rose Garden

There Are No Victims!

"Everyone has a point of view and then they spend all of their waking time looking for evidence to support that point of view."
Michael Gerber

I'd love to tell you how I have learned that there are no victims and that I live my life knowing that I create the world in which I live. But I can't. I'm not there yet. One of the major reasons I am writing this book is because I feel like a victim when it comes to writing. Ten years ago, I was asked to write an article for an association I had spoken for. The editor told me that I was a better speaker than writer. Then I wrote the first draft of this book more than three years ago and sent it to an editor, who reviewed it, sent it back, and told me that it had to be rewritten. I took that to mean that I was a lousy writer, so I shelved the book, and I rested my case. I had all the evidence I needed to believe I was not a writer. How many times has this or something similar happened to you? I believe that we are not victims. I believe we have control over our thoughts and that those thoughts create the world we live in every day.

We live in a world that labels us as "victims" when unfortunate things happen to us. Therefore, it's very easy for us to believe that when life doesn't go the way we want it to go, we are victims of circumstances beyond our control. The advantages of this belief system are that we don't have to accept responsibility for our thoughts or actions, we get to be just like everyone else who believes that they are victims, we feel helpless and powerless, we get to stay stuck in our familiar lives, and we get to continue to play small.

A logical question to ask is, "What am I learning by believing that I am a victim?" Some of the answers might be: "I'm learning to be hostile and resentful. I'm learning not to trust people. I'm withdrawn, and many times, I see my life situation as hopeless. I often feel helpless. I feel misunderstood. I'm skeptical, critical, judgmental, negative and fearful. I'm scared and vengeful." I'm sure you have your own list of things you've learned from believing that you are a victim.

However, these are very heavy burdens that we're carrying. What has your victim mentality cost you emotionally, physically, financially, professionally and spiritually? Have you paid a high enough price yet for being a victim? If not, how much more will you pay before you are ready to give up the role of victim?

What are some of the disadvantages of our believing that we are victims? We never get the opportunity to learn lessons. We don't grow. We don't reach our full potential. Others never benefit from our divine gifts because we believe we are victims. We stay stuck, and our lives become like the movie *Groundhog Day*, where the main character keeps repeating the same day over and over again. What are some of the disadvantages that you see in your life when you choose to see yourself as a victim?

If you feel you have paid enough in your life, you can now choose to step into the role of being the creator of your life! When you accept that you have the power to choose how you think in every situation, your life begins to change in innumerable ways. You forgive others and yourself for events over which you thought you had no control. You let go of the past. You release all of the emotions you have stored inside. You reclaim your power, and you begin the process of taking responsibility for the outcomes in your life.

Let's look at some ramifications of choosing to believe that you can be the creator of your life. The first thing you have to do is give up

A Rose Garden

feeling sorry for yourself because your life is such a mess. You created this mess because you didn't know you had the ability to create it. Now that you know all that you can create, you should be excited about it—not upset about what you created when you had no conscious idea of what you were doing. You can begin to dream again, because you know now that you have the power to create whatever you want in your life. You reclaim your power, because you are no longer willing to accept that you are a victim of anything or anyone. You are not afraid to use your power, because you know that you will not abuse your power. You will use it to create a better life for yourself and others. I now have the freedom to fulfill my life mission. I have given myself permission to be all that I can be. What an incredible gift you can give to yourself by releasing the need to feel like a victim and assuming responsibility for creating the life of your dreams!

Choosing not to see yourself as a victim is not a one-time event. It is a process that you must continue choosing on an ongoing basis. Tell yourself, "I create my life every single moment of every single day!"

Exercise:

Write down one thing that you would like to create in your life. What thoughts do you have to repeat in your mind in order for this goal to become a reality? Write these thoughts down on a three by five card, along with your goal, and carry it with you everywhere you go. Read these thoughts every chance you get—at least ten times a day until your goal is realized.

Affirmation:

I am the creator of my life!

You Are A Spiritual Being

"You are not a human being having a spiritual experience. You are a spiritual being having a human experience." Dr. Wayne Dyer

Almost all religions teach that the essence of life is the soul or the spirit. The premise is that the soul exists before its time in the body and after the time in the body. Some call it spirit. We acknowledge on an intellectual level that we are spiritual beings, however, when we come into this physical body, it seems like we totally forget that there's a spiritual being in here.

Many identify who we are in life by what our tasks are. If I were to ask you the question who are you, how would you answer it? Would you say "I'm a..." and give the title of your job, or the title of your profession? Would you say your name, and "I'm a stay-at-home mom?" Would you say "I'm a race car driver," or "I'm a speaker," or "I'm an author"? How would you answer the question?

How would your life change if you identified yourself as a spiritual being? Your purpose as a spiritual being would be to come into this physical body. While you are in your physical body, you will undergo certain experiences that will enable you to develop a deeper sense of yourself and to have physical experiences that are impossible without a body. Without the body, all these experiences would be nothing but a philosophical discussion. When you recognize the reason for your physicality is to gain a wealth of experiences, you are less afraid of these experiences. Instead, you have the strength, courage, and confidence to face them knowing that this was why you came to visit this body in the first place.

Envision that there are two people living inside of you competing for control of how you process the events of your physical existence.

A Rose Garden

The first person is the ego, and his responsibility is to interpret every event in your life in such a way that you are in a constant state of chaos. The second person is your higher self. His job is to interpret every event in your life in such a way as it brings you a sense of peace. The way you know who is running your life at any particular time is to determine whether you are in a state of chaos or peace.

The ego is loud, domineering, pushy, aggressive and very intimidating. Your higher self is very soft-spoken. It waits for you to ask for its assistance before it responds. Then you must be very attentive to hear what it suggests. The easiest way to know when it is present is when you feel a sense of peace. To invoke the higher self ask: if I want peace in my life, how do I need to interpret this event?

You wouldn't be reading this book if at some level you do not agree with the concept that you are a spiritual being. The challenge now is to become more intimately associated with the qualities of your spirit being.

Exercise:

Go back to your favorite spot in your mind. Have two seats that are extraordinary beautiful, plush and comfortable. Go into your meditative state, invite your spirit being to come and sit in the chair. Ask it, how can I get to know you better? Listen for the answer. Record the answer and when you're satisfied with the answer, thank your spirit being. Your spirit being has a gift for you. Thank your spirit being for the gift. Open the gift and know how you are to use that gift. If you cannot or do not know how to use the gift ask your spirit being how it wants you to use the gift.

Affirmation:

I embrace my spiritual being.

There's Enough to Go Around

"We cannot hold a torch to light another's path without brightening our own." Ben Sweetland

We live in a world that is overflowing with abundance, yet nearly all of us believe that we live in a world where there isn't enough to go around. Therefore, many of us hoard and refuse to share. There is an abundance of money and natural resources. There is absolutely enough of everything for everyone. The belief in scarcity is one of the most toxic beliefs on the planet. A belief in scarcity causes us to believe that we should be suspicious of others because they will steal our share, that there is only one pie and that everything we get means someone else gets less. This belief makes our lives ones of fear, tension, apprehension, distrust, skepticism and unrest.

How would your life change if you believed that there was enough for everyone to have everything they wanted? You would share your knowledge, material resources, money, gifts and everything else that you have. Fear, distrust and unrest would disappear and be replaced by love, acceptance, trust, understanding, peace and harmony. The choice is yours. Do you choose a life of abundance or scarcity?

Remember that when you change your belief from one of scarcity to one of abundance, your external circumstances won't change immediately. You will have to have faith and trust and know that abundance is on its way. In the meantime, share what you have, knowing that more is on the way. Giving and receiving are the same. Begin the process of giving and sharing everything you have with the knowledge that there is an unlimited supply and that you will receive your share of that infinite supply.

A Rose Garden

Recessions and depressions happen when the flow of money is slowed down. People get scared. They say, "Oh my God, something bad might happen, so I'll sell my stock, I won't buy a new car, I won't buy a new house, I won't buy a new washing machine." In other words, they adopt the belief of scarcity. When we stop the flow of money, people who produce the goods and services we ordinarily purchase lose their jobs. They slow down their purchases, and then more people lose their jobs, and the cycle continues. The key is to not allow fear to govern your life.

A real gift is given without any expectation of how the other person will receive it or what he or she will do with it. When you have an expectation, you are not giving a gift, because expectation is really nothing more than premeditated resentment. When you give with expectations attached, you are basically lending something to someone and telling him by your actions and/or your words how he is supposed to use the gift in order to gain your approval. Your life will flow when you give fully and freely of everything you have, with the faith that it will contribute to the quality of life for all of us and be returned to you to an even greater degree.

Whatever your profession, give freely and teach the people in it everything you have learned from your years of experience. Do this without any fear that they could possibly take your job or money or standard of living away from you. Give of yourself with the vision of contributing to the betterment of society, and you will benefit from a society that functions at a higher level. If each of us had the goal of raising the consciousness of everyone whose lives we touched, the world would be a magnificent place in which to live.

There is nothing to be afraid of. Our essence—that is, who we really are—is a spiritual being. We have chosen to come into our physical bodies to learn lessons. My essence is who I am. It has nothing to do with the body I'm in, what it looks like or how it functions. My body may take a beating physically, mentally and psychologically; however, that's not who I am. I am an incredible divine being in this dense environment, trying to learn the experiences and lessons of this world. One of the most important lessons is that we're all here together, and everything we have is here to be shared.

Exercise:

Think of one area of your life that you would like to share with other people, whether it's your professional area of expertise or charity work. Where could you share the gifts that have been given to you? Develop a plan to expand your vision of what sharing means and how it will impact your life and the lives of everyone you touch. All of us have skipped a stone across a pond and watched the ripples spread across the water. Throw your stone into the pond of life and see how sharing your gifts, money and talent will have a ripple effect on the entire world.

Affirmation:

I live in a world overflowing with abundance. Everything I have, I share with everyone who touches my life.

A Rose Garden

You Always Do the Best You Can With the Resources You Have Available

"To be thrown upon one's own resources is to be cast into the very lap of fortune: For our faculties then undergo a development and display an energy of which they were previously unsusceptible."
Benjamin Franklin

We always do the best we can do with the resources we have available to us at any given moment. Sometimes we have resources that allow us to move mountains, and other times, those resources hardly allow us to get out of bed.

If you were standing near a swimming pool and the person you loved most in the world was drowning, nothing could stop you from jumping into that pool and attempting to save that person. You'd jump in the pool even if you didn't know how to swim. This is a time when your resources would make you unstoppable.

Think about an event that really depressed you, that made you feel like you couldn't take any action at all. What happened was that you were not able to get to the resources that were available to you to take a higher, more productive action. But that was the best that you could do with the resources that were available at that moment. For whatever reason, there may not have been any resources available to you because you were scared, angry, depressed or whatever. Accept that you did the best you could with what you had available to you at that time.

The key is to know the resources that are available and what you need to do in order to access them. What would your mindset be if you jumped into the pool? It probably would be that you had to do whatever was necessary to save this person. You wouldn't give any consideration to your personal safety or whether or not you could swim. You would never think about what your limitations were.

What would happen if you used that resource to get a job or solve a problem in a relationship? Your laser vision would enable you to pursue the situation the same way you would pursue the drowning person. Your health wouldn't be an issue, you wouldn't consider your well-being, you'd have absolutely no fear, and you would do whatever you had to do to handle the situation.

On the other hand, when your resources barely allow you to get out of bed, what happens? You are not able to access the resource of being unstoppable. But you do the best you can with the resources you are able to access. This is true for every human being in every situation. With this understanding, it is easier to forgive people who have wronged you. You now understand that they did the very best they could with the resources they were able to access at that moment. This knowledge enables us to forgive our parents for whatever terrible things they did to us.

How do you access your resources? One way is to change your physiology. You've got to create energy in your body; you've got to create force. Change the way you see the situation. Raise your head up, throw your shoulders back and tell yourself you can do it. Take some kind of action. The key is to be able to insert a second in between the event and the action. In that second, ask yourself what you would do if you were in a state of total resourcefulness.

Exercise:

Think of an instance when someone did something offensive to you. See every detail of the situation. How was he breathing? What did he say? What did he do? What did you say? What did you do? What were you thinking? What resources would you give the other

A Rose Garden

person and yourself to handle the situation differently? Go back and re-create every detail of the event, but this time, equip yourself and the other person with the resources necessary to create the outcome you want. I promise that as you replay the event, you will get a different result. The event exists only as a perception in your mind. You have the ability to give yourself and the other person the gifts necessary to change the outcome that exists only in your mind. Forgive yourself and the other person.

Affirmation:

I love myself for always doing the best I can do and constantly finding new ways to use the resources I have available to me.

You Are Not the General Manager of the World

"Do I want to experience peace or do I want to experience conflict?"
Jerry Jampolsky

One of the things that causes us so much anxiety is getting upset about things over which we have no control. I have a long list in this category: a stoplight turning red every time I get there, the way other people drive, poor customer service, long lines, people putting their luggage over my seat on an airplane or the person in front of me on an airplane reclining his seat and smashing my knees. I could go on and on, but you get the idea. Each one of us has a list of things that constitutes our beliefs about how life should work. When things don't go right, we feel a tremendous amount of anxiety. The challenge is to let go.

I love the Serenity Prayer: "God grant me the serenity to accept the things I cannot change, the courage to change the things I can, and the wisdom to know the difference."

During one of my cruise ship speaking engagements, a woman (whom I will call Mary) shared that she had provided foster care for more than 400 children. One of the children she adopted is now a lesbian, and based on Mary's religious beliefs, Mary could not accept her daughter's sexual orientation. This created tremendous pressure for Mary. Her religion, which she loved, told her that lesbians were unacceptable. She also loved her daughter, but because her daughter did not conform to her religious beliefs, she felt estranged from her. I suggested to Mary that she give me her written resignation as general manager of the world. She did that and felt a tremendous sense of relief. She now has permission to love her daughter and her religion both, without her daughter having to conform to her specific religious

A Rose Garden

beliefs.

We have all written our own versions of the book called *Life According to Me*. When we're young, we're constantly looking for data that will tell us how life works. Years later, however, we suddenly conclude that we know it all! We then stop receiving data about how life could work. That's when we start to see life through the "life according to me" filter. Instinctively, we know that no one else in the whole world sees life the way we do, but we still have the expectation that life should work according to our beliefs and values. When it doesn't, we try to control it. When we're unable to control it and get the outcomes we believe are right, we get frustrated.

This is a massive problem. There are billions of people on this planet who believe that everyone should see life, behave and think according to their own values and beliefs. Virtually all religious wars arise because one group of people doesn't believe what the other group believes. One country invades another country because of differing cultures. Often, when other people are different from us, we get scared, and the only way we know how to deal with that intense fear is to lash out.

We must learn to live together with our differences. No one else in the world sees life the way we do, but we all want others to accept us just the way we are. In order for us to have the freedom to be the way we are, we must first accept others just as they are.

Before that can happen, we must first accept ourselves just the way we are. Then we must stop trying to control other people and circumstances in our lives. We must stop thinking that we know best how someone else should think, behave or believe. It is our responsibility to be who we are and continue to strive to become all that we possibly can. Every other human being's life is an agreement between him and his Creator, and we have no right to interfere in that relationship. Our responsibility is to focus on our relationship with our Creator and move in the direction of fulfilling the purpose that we came here to fulfill. Then we can support and love other people as they strive to fulfill the purposes of their lives.

Most of us don't even know the purposes of our own lives, let alone the purpose of someone else's. What I'm trying to get across here is that we need to spend all our life's energy and attention getting to know our own life purpose and then fulfilling it. When we do that, the next step is to allow everyone else in our lives that same freedom.

I guarantee that if you focus your attention on discovering and fulfilling your purpose, and loving and supporting everyone else in their journey to discover and fulfill their life purpose, yours will be fulfilled. There will be a tremendous sense of relief when you stop trying to get other people to live the way you think they ought to live. Love them just the way they are and love yourself just the way you are. You are perfect just the way you are, and they are perfect just the way they are.

Exercise:

Think of one person whom you need to allow to live the way he chooses. Write him a letter apologizing for being so arrogant as to think that you know what is right for him. Thank him for being a great teacher to you, and tell him that you know that he is in great hands—God's. Release him to a life of love and fulfillment as he journeys through his life. After you've completed this letter, re-read it and tear it up.

Affirmation:

I embrace my life as a physical experience with God on earth. I allow every human being to live his or her life as an expression of God.

A Rose Garden

Whatever You Resist Persists

"Life at any time can become difficult. Life at any time can become easy. It all depends upon how one adjusts oneself to life."
Morarji Desai

We resist the things we don't like. But the lesson is that everything we resist continues to plague us. In order to get rid of what we are resisting, we must embrace it. Because we are so used to resisting things that upset us, it goes against our instincts to embrace them. Additionally, we must be willing to accept that this is the way things will be for the rest of our lives. We have to stop fighting things and learn to flow with life. We must learn to live life on life's terms. I know this concept sticks in your throat, but we are here to learn, and this is one of the most important lessons there is. The fact that you are resisting something may be a clue that you haven't learned the lesson you need to learn in that matter. But life will become a lot easier when you do.

Most of us are control freaks. When we resist, we struggle, and when we stop resisting, we let go. My favorite prayer is, "Let go. Let God." One of the most significant lessons I have learned from yoga is that when I am struggling with a pose and I am trying to muscle into it, the most effective thing I can do is relax my breathing. It amazes me how every time I do, my whole body automatically relaxes and goes deeper into the pose. When we resist something, we are denying that our lives are part of a divine plan and that it is happening for our own good.

One of my favorite quotes from *A Course in Miracles* is, "What could you not accept if you but knew that everything that happens to you in your life… is gently planned by one whose only purpose is your good?" (Workbook, p. 247 1st edition p. 255 2nd edition) That means that everything that happens to me in my life is a gift from God. If I trust in God and His love for me, then I am essentially saying, "Okay, God. This really doesn't look like, feel like or taste like a gift, but because I believe in you and trust in you, I accept that this is a gift."

My next question is, "How is a difficult situation a gift?" When I get quiet and keep asking how, the answers come. This enables me to relax and accept a situation, knowing that it is part of my life plan. Everyone's parents have said, "Some day you will understand" or "I am doing this for your own good." I know that God is constantly saying to us, "Honey, some day you will understand."

We always have choices, and we are finding all kinds of ways to give up our power. By resisting, we deprive ourselves of the opportunity to learn one of the lessons we came here to learn. When we resist, we don't believe that we have any choices.

I once worked with someone who was going home to visit her dad. She was dreading the visit, because to her, he was a real pain. She felt powerless to counter his negative emotions and didn't realize that she had any choices about how she could react to his behavior. I suggested that she see him as an actor in a movie and watch him give an Academy Award-winning performance, playing the part of a jerk. She did exactly that and had the best visit she'd ever had with him. She stopped resisting his personality and just said, "Wow! He is doing a great job of playing the role he has played all of his life."

When you do this, you are surrendering to the process of life. You are not trying to control it, and you cease trying to be the general manager of the world. There is a tremendous freedom that comes when we stop resisting. The best thing that happens is you gain a tremendous sense of peace. It's like the song that Perry Como sang years ago: "Que sera, sera. Whatever will be will be."

A Rose Garden

Exercise:

Make a list of all the things in your life that you are resisting. Pick one that you would like to confront. How are you being served by resisting this? What is good about this situation? What do you have to believe in order to embrace the situation? What actions do you have to take to embrace the situation?

Affirmation:

I surrender to the divine plan for my life. Everything that happens in my life is for my highest good.

Your Past Doesn't Have to Determine Your Present

"Life is divided into three times—that which was, which is, and which will be. Let us learn from the past to profit by the present, and from the present to live better in the future." William Wordsworth

Life is always filled with new challenges. When a problem presents itself in our lives, we often look at how we can solve it. But all too often, we look back at prior unsuccessful experiences and say, "I failed at this before, so I probably will again."

Failure is a point of view. We all have our own definitions of failure. What if your definition of failure was, "The only time I can fail is when I don't try"? Then, whenever you tried something you would be successful!

What we do, however, is equate past failures with present circumstances. We think that life is a mathematical equation: Yesterday = Today = Tomorrow. In other words, The Past = The Present = The Future. "If I couldn't do it yesterday, I can't do it today, and I won't be able to do it tomorrow."

It is amazing how many ways we find to give our power away. By using past unsuccessful experiences as our guideline, we are powerless. You are not the person you were when a past event occurred. You learned something from that event. What was it?

Dwelling on the past has no productive value today. Today, you can say, "I am" or "I can." Simply declare in your mind that you have the ability to successfully solve the challenge at hand. In sales, the saying is "Act as if." In other words, act as if you have successfully managed a situation hundreds of times before. Do you ever get up out of a chair, thinking, "How am I going to walk? I'm not sure that I can walk"?

A Rose Garden

Absolutely not. It is so much a part of who you are that you don't even give it a conscious thought. Have that same conviction and confidence about every challenge and problem that faces you in life. You do not have to have prior experience at something in order for you to be able to successfully solve it now.

There is a divine consciousness that knows how to solve every situation in our lives. All we have to do is to tap into it. How? Talk to God like you would talk to your best friend. Once you have asked Him to help you solve a problem, listen for the answer. One way is to meditate. Another is to understand how God works. He may not send the answer to you directly. It may come to you through another person. You may read the answer in a book or magazine. You may see it in a TV show or movie. The point is that once you have asked for help, you must constantly be aware that the answer to your problem may come from anywhere, including a dream.

Another suggestion is to hire yourself as a consultant to solve the problem. You may ask what difference that will make. If you are looking at the problem as a consultant, you are much more objective about it. Your emotions won't cloud your ability to come up with a successful solution.

Use your past experiences to help you solve current problems and challenges. However, when past experiences become a hindrance, discard them. They have no value. It is like eating ripe fruit and throwing away rotten fruit. If it doesn't serve you, discard it!

I think of myself as a speaker, not a writer. But then I took a class on developing self-awareness and e-mailed a draft of this manuscript to one of the teachers, who told me to take it out of mothballs and finalize it. She also said I was an amazing man. I have no idea what that referred to specifically, but I loved hearing it, and now I have all the evidence I need to finish this book and get it published.

When I meditate about this book, I am guided to surrender to the lessons in growth that I will experience by going through the processes of writing and publishing. What stories from your past have you used as evidence to convince yourself that you can't do something? Are you ready to face your fears and go through them and dispel them forever? You are not your past.

Exercise:

Think of a situation that is unresolved in your life right now. Identify what is stopping you from successfully solving this problem or challenge. Tap into the universal consciousness and ask for the perfect solution. Then very calmly go about your daily life, being aware that the solution may present itself in the most unsuspecting place. Keep a notebook with you to jot down the answers, because they may come in bits and pieces. Also ask for the answers in a dream.

Affirmation:

All of my power is in the present moment.

A Rose Garden

We Are All in Life Together

"I believe that you can get everything in life you want if you will just help enough other people get what they want." Zig Ziglar

Often, we humans interact with each other as if we're mortal enemies. We abuse the people that we live with and love by speaking harshly to them, not respecting them and not looking for the precious gifts they have. We don't respect the differences in the people we live with or work with because of their personalities, their cultural differences, their backgrounds, etc. We talk nastily to people in grocery stores, department stores, airline counters, and we look down on people who we think have jobs that are beneath us.

It doesn't really matter what our job titles are, what our monetary status is. We are all in this life together. We all live on the planet Earth, we all breathe the same oxygen and drink the same water, and therefore, we need to share all of the resources that we have and ensure that they are available to future generations. All of us want to be respected. We achieve respect when we respect others, regardless of our differences.

Who is your enemy? Is it someone who insulted you or hurt you physically? Is it someone who has a different skin color, a different religion, a different belief? What would your life be like if everyone respected you, no matter how different you were from them? The change would be enormous! How does it start? It starts with you accepting people just the way they are.

You may be thinking, "What about rapists or murders?" While there may be some exceptions, let's look at how we can change the world by changing our attitudes about most people in our lives.

Others are simply mirrors of ourselves. If other people reflect to us our unresolved issues, then there are no enemies, only teachers! Learn to embrace yourself, to accept the shortcomings you have. When you accept your shortcomings, it's much easier to accept others just the way they are. They are just a different aspect of you. Each of us has a unique way of seeing life. The most important thing to realize is that we're all living life together.

We all have similar goals. We want to be happy, we want a sense of peace, we want to be successful in our lives (however we define success), and we want to be able to do the things we want. In Gary Zukav's book *Soul Stories*, the author says, "Life is a one-room school house." When I think of a one-room school house, I think of kids of all ages taking care of each other. The older ones are taking care of and teaching the younger ones, and some day the younger kids will grow up and take care of the younger students. Similarly, when we were born, we were totally dependent upon our parents. Often, later, our parents become completely dependent on us.

It seems to me that crises and natural disasters bring out the best in people. That's when we stop being selfish and reach out to other people who are much needier, without any concern about our own safety or our needs. We know that they need us to help them to get through tough times. That's what life is about, supporting each other when we need it. We're all here together, we all have different skills, and we all have different traits. One is no better or worse than another. Effectively, we are all one family that needs to take care of itself.

Exercise:

Determine what your gifts are and volunteer your time to mentor someone in your area of expertise. Watch how that person's life changes because you cared enough to make a difference.

A Rose Garden

Affirmation:

Life is incredibly beautiful. I live for the expression and the experience of the magnificence of life. And everywhere I go and everyone I meet, I search for their magnificence and their beauty. I always find what I am looking for.

Everyone is a Winner

"Triumph is made up of two words: 'try' and 'umph.'"
(from *The Little Book of Hope* by Robert H. Schuller)

We live in a world of duality: hot and cold, right and wrong, good and bad, winner and loser, short and tall, top and bottom, inside and outside. Most of us have been programmed to believe that we are not winners and that if you aren't a winner, then you are a loser.

The dictionary defines a winner as a successful person. If my definition of success is, "I am a success when I am alive," then I am always a success! If I define success as any time I try, then whenever I try, I am a success.

Most of us interpret the events in our lives and give them meaning based on our perceptions. Simply accept that you are a success and that you don't have to do anything special to be a winner. I declare that you are a winner and a success by virtue of the fact that you are alive. You can choose to believe me, or you can believe that you must attain some high standard to be successful. You do that for a short period of time and then you must prove yourself all over again. Which belief do you choose?

Exercise:

For the next week, write down every reason why God knows you are a winner. In a leisurely way, review this list three times a day. Savor it. You have just had your true identity revealed to you by your creator. Believe Him and live your life with that knowledge.

Affirmation:

I am a winner.

A Rose Garden

You Will Die

"Life is the childhood of our immortality." Johann W. Goethe

We all know we're going to die. So what is the lesson in knowing it? You may intellectually know it as a fact, but you don't live your life in accordance with that knowledge. In order to fully appreciate life to its fullest, you cannot live with the fear of dying today. Live as if today were the last day of your life. If that were true, could you say that you had no regrets? You are writing the story of your life. Is it the story you want it to be? If not, now is the time to change the script. If today were your last day, whom would you call to say, "I'm sorry" or "Forgive me" or "Thanks for being such an incredible person and having such an impact in my life"?

Treat life as if it were the most sacred and precious possession you will ever receive. It is! People tend to remember their most recent experience with someone. What do you want that memory to be? Let's say that you dine at an exquisite restaurant but you get sick because the cream in the dessert is spoiled. What will be your memory of the experience? It probably won't be of the incredible meal but of getting sick. Treat every interaction as if you were creating the last memory that a person will have of you.

When you look back on your life, do you want to see only on a series of memories that just *happened*? Why not actively create these memories for yourself and those who love you? What greater tribute could there be than an intentional life? Live your life fully. Don't be afraid of what people will think of you or say about you. Create your legacy. What do you want people to say about your life and how it touched them? Live consciously. Touch people's lives in the deepest and most sincere way you possible can. Come from a place of intention.

Live your life proactively, not reactively.

Live your life with the four qualities of a baby: Love unconditionally, forgive and forget, see everything in your life as an adventure, and have no concept of failure. Hold on to dear friendships, cherish people and experiences, look for something to love about everyone you ever meet, enjoy the adventure of your life, and know that you can never fail.

Now you are ready to live fully, live gracefully and be yourself. You are the only person who has ever received the gifts you have. Please share them with everyone you meet.

Exercise:

Find a quiet place where you will not be disturbed. Take several deep breaths and relax. Fast forward your life to your last day on earth. Where are you? Are you in a bed, sleeping or sick? Are you in a car or going about your day-to-day activities? Who is with you? If there is pain, feel it. Use all of your senses. What do you smell? What is the energy like in the room? Is there love or fear? If there are people with you, what are they saying to you and what are they thinking? Say all of your goodbyes if there are people with you. It is time to take your last breath. Are you afraid, or are you at peace? Now that your life has expired, what happens to you? Where are you going? What does the air look like? Is there music? How does it feel? Are there smells? Describe them. Notice every last detail. Who is coming to meet you? Feel the ecstasy. Heighten your sensual awareness. You are recording every last detail. You notice everything, and time is standing still.

You have now experienced your death, and faced the experience as if it was real. Now come back into the present. Gently open your eyes. Welcome back to the world of the body. Enjoy every moment you have left. Take the time to write down everything you experienced in

A Rose Garden

this enactment of your death. Now that you have gone through the experience of your death you are no longer afraid to die and can live fully. You have a template for the happiest and most successful life you can live. Read this over and over until you can live with the heartbeat that pulses with this message. It is your life line. These are not words; they are a road map to an incredible life.

Affirmation:

I live only in the present moment and enjoy every moment of my life.

Part 2

Attitudes That Will Minimize Life's Struggles

A Rose Garden

Life Is a Perception

"Reflect that life like every other blessing derives its value from its use alone." Samuel Johnson

The author of *A Course in Miracles* outlines two important facts about perception: "Nothing I see in this room (on this street, from this window, in this place) means anything" and "I have given everything I see in this room (on this street, from this window, in this place) all the meaning it has for me" (Workbook, p. 4, 2nd edition). This means that events only have the meaning we choose to give them.

If we accept as fact that nothing has any meaning, then it's easy to accept that everything we see, touch and experience in life is a perception. In other words, there's another way to look at a situation, no matter what it is. Often, we don't form favorable perceptions of people, events or even our own past actions. Our interpretations take us to the worst-case scenario, because we see ourselves as limited, fearful, frustrated, incapable people.

In 1996, my wife, Rosemarie, was the chairperson of a pharmacy convention. The couple in charge of the education program, Chuck and Theresa, wanted me to give the keynote speech, but the convention board said no because my speaking might be perceived as a conflict of interest.

My perception at the time was that this was terrible, because I had spoken for that association four previous times. But because I was not allowed to give the keynote speech, I developed a relationship with Chuck, and he subsequently became my best friend. In other words, if I had given a keynote speech, Chuck and I would probably still just be casual acquaintances today.

The challenge is to change your perceptions when they don't serve you. Your goal is to recognize when your ego is in control of your life. You know the ego is in control when you are in a state of unrest, chaos, frustration or anger. Learn to recognize when the ego is present and say, "Please step aside so I may find my inner peace." Invite Spirit in, and ask Spirit to give you a higher perception of the meaning of a particular event, which will give you a sense of peace. Spirit is always there and available to you at any time to give you the gift of true perception, the ability to see how an event fits into your life and the scheme of life as a whole.

Exercise:

Identify one area of your life with which you are struggling. Meditate about it. Invite Spirit to come to you. Ask Spirit to give you the true meaning of the event. Once you feel a complete sense of peace, thank Spirit. As Spirit leaves, ask it to give you a gift. Ask Spirit how to use this gift in your life.

Affirmation:

I am thrilled to have Spirit as my partner to give to me the true perception of the events in my life.

A Rose Garden

You Are the Only Person Who Sees Life the Way You Do

"There is nothing either good or bad, but thinking makes it so."
William Shakespeare

As I mentioned in an earlier chapter, each of us has written an unpublished book titled *Life According To Me*. When we're young, we observe life and learn from our experiences. We attach meanings to different things and develop conclusions about those things. At some point, when we get a little older, we stop accepting new data and suddenly conclude that we know how life works. We think we know how relationships will work, how far we will go in our careers, how much money we will make, etc. This causes us to have rigid attitudes about how life works. This is when we begin the process of dying.

In order to be happy in life, it's very important to understand that everyone sees life differently than you do; no other human being sees life the way you do. If we're going to get along with people, if we're going to learn, if we're going to expand and grow, then it's mandatory that we be open and flexible to seeing how others see life, because to them, that's the only way life exists. It doesn't make them right, and it doesn't make them wrong. But because we love others, because we respect them, because they are our fellow human beings, we owe it to them and to ourselves to see life from their point of view, even if we don't agree with it.

However, when we acknowledge that everyone sees life differently than we do and we're open to the possibility that there's another way to view any situation (and we all know there is), we expand our horizons. We're able to bring in new ways of viewing situations that we previously found unacceptable. Through their worldview, others give us the opportunities to find new ways to look at our lives, and in many instances, they're going to be there to help us release the desire to see life only through our lenses.

In addition, if we are open to hearing how other people see things, they are more likely to respect our different views. It is fascinating how we understand that we are the only ones who see our lives the way we do, yet we are always trying to convert people to our way. Look at all the misery and death this has caused: holy wars, conflicts between Protestants and Catholics, Jews and Palestinians, the rise of Hitler and the Aryan race, and the list goes on and on. We are all fine just the way we are. We need to accept ourselves just the way we are and then accept other people just the way they are. Let's release the need to convert the world to our own ways. If we were all meant to look the same, think the same, act the same and like the same things, then we would have been created to all be alike. We weren't. It is our challenge to find the beauty in being different.

I am convinced that we are here to learn from each other. If we are trying to make everyone else like ourselves, how will we ever learn anything? If our way is the only way, then we must be living perfect lives. But if life has its problems, and all of our lives do, then we need to turn to each other and listen to how things are going in each other's lives. If we can ask, "How does the other person sees this?" then we have a chance to learn and grow. My father-in-law used to tell me that we have two ears and one mouth so we can listen twice as much as we talk. It has also been said that if a man keeps his mouth shut and listens, others may think he is a fool, but if he opens his mouth, they will know it for sure.

Imagine that your job in life is to gather data on how other people perceive that life works. In order to be successful at this you will have to

A Rose Garden

objectively listen to how others see life. One of the tools you will bring into this interaction is the desire to be inquisitive and the willingness to say: " I never thought of it that way." It requires bringing an open mind.. Albert Einstein said, "You can never solve a problem on the level on which it was created."

My wife is always is showing me another way to look at things, which frustrates me. Now my challenge is to say to others, "That's another way to look at it." When we acknowledge that people come to us as our teachers, we release the need to control their lives. In our graciousness, we accept that others come into our lives to teach us another way to do something.

Exercise:

Identify one area of your life in which you have a strong opinion. The next time you have a conversation with someone on that topic, ask him his opinion and then listen to his point of view. When you're listening, try not to get too emotionally attached to your point of view. The other person is not attacking your identity or your point of view. He is just sharing a point of view about a particular subject. Now you have the opportunity to review or perhaps revise your point of view about that subject. If you're having difficulty listening because you're too attached to your point of view, imagine yourself sitting in a theater watching the two of you having this conversation. The goal is to get to the point where you can have such a discussion without feeling that your identity as a human being is being attacked.

Affirmation:

I embrace opposing points of view as my greatest teacher in my growth and development as a student of life on planet Earth.

Have an Attitude of Gratitude!*

> "O praise His goodness with songs for thanksgiving,
> And meditate in silence on the wonders of His Love;
> Let thy heart overflow with gratitude and acknowledgement,
> Let the language of thy lips speak praise and adoration,
> Let the actions of thy life show thy love to His law."
> Akhenaton

Several years ago, I injured my Achilles tendon. I limped and was in pain for more than seven months. When it healed, I was so grateful to be able to walk without a limp and without pain. During that period, I noticed how many people walked with a limp, and I felt compassion for them.

One January, I had a bad cold and was taking a cold remedy to help me breathe. But I could only use it every eight hours. When the medicine worked, I would say a prayer of thanks. I was so grateful to be able to breathe. It was the first time in my life that I had felt gratitude for my breath. Imagine—breathing is one of the most vital aspects of my life, and I had never given thanks for it! What an attitude! It showed a total lack of appreciation.

I used to live in Chicago, where we had some really long, cold winters. I remember going out to a tree in the back yard one spring and holding a branch and marveling at how it had come back to life. Nature has so many incredible splendors that she gives us: sunrises, sunsets, flowers, trees, mountains, lakes, oceans, fruits and vegetables. Our environment is the source of life. Not only is it our responsibility to be grateful for it, we must respect it and do everything possible to ensure that we sustain it for future generations. We have no right to pollute it or destroy it. Show your gratitude by taking care of this

A Rose Garden

precious gift.

How much time do you spend being grateful? Maybe you could spend a few minutes contemplating your gratitude from time to time. You could express gratitude for being alive, living where you do, your health, the gifts you have, your career, your home, your family, the weather, your neighbors, your car, living in a democracy, and the list goes on and on.

We all need to develop a deeper sense of gratitude for all of the tremendous gifts we have. We have more material possessions now than during any other time in history. And in the U.S., we have more material things than any other country in the world. However, we have so much that it is easy to take it all for granted. Develop the habit of being grateful for all that comes to you in your life, no matter how big or small it is. It only takes a second. First, give thanks within yourself, and then if someone did something for you, tell her how grateful you are. And say it from the bottom of your heart.

Developing a sincere sense of gratitude enhances your appreciation of life and enables you to live a much fuller existence with what you have right now. We live in a society that never has enough. When you express your gratitude for everything you have in your life, you stop continuously wanting more. You realize how rich and abundant your life is today, even if you never gain one more thing! A sincere practice of gratitude will give you a life of abundance. It's not what you have that matters but what you appreciate. We are incredibly wealthy. All we have to do is make the time to take an inventory of this wealth and be grateful for it. What we are grateful for multiplies.

Exercise:

Start the custom of regularly sending someone a note telling her how grateful you are to have her in your life. Tell her how she makes a difference. Imagine how this simple gesture will change the world. If you send fifty of these notes a year and only ten percent of these people start the habit themselves, imagine how many people's lives will be enriched and how this will change our own attitudes about life and everyone we encounter. For one week, every time you see someone, ask yourself, "What am I grateful to this person for?"

Affirmation:

I constantly express my gratitude for everyone and everything in my life.

(Footnotes)
*From <u>Attitudes of Gratitude</u> by M.J. Ryan

A Rose Garden

Accept Responsibility for Everything That Happens to You

"Faced with crisis, the man of character falls back on himself. He improves his own stamp of action, takes responsibility for it and makes it his own." Charles De Gaulle

The opposite of having a victim's mentality is accepting responsibility for creating everything that you have in your life. It amazes me how many ways we find to make ourselves victim. Avoiding the victim mentality is another way to take responsibility for creating everything that happens to you. When something upsetting occurs, rather than allowing your ego to upset you, ask instead, "How did I create this? How does this serve me?"

Maybe you are being served in a negative way. I know a person who is overweight because she's afraid of men. Being overweight enables her to not be attractive to men, and therefore, accomplish her unconscious goal of keeping men away.

Once you have accepted responsibility for creating what happens in your life, you are much more powerful, because rather than seeing yourself as a victim of some arbitrary force, you know there is something in your thinking and in your beliefs that attracts negative circumstances into your life. To ensure that you don't create them again, ask yourself what you would have to believe in order to create those circumstances in your life. This may be painful. You're not going to change until the pain you're in exceeds the pain of looking at how your negative thinking creates misfortune. If you're not able to see how you're sabotaging yourself, ask a friend to help you.

By accepting responsibility for everything in your life, you reclaim your power! Now you have the ability to look at your life and ask,

"What do I need to change about the way I think of myself or what I believe?" As an analogy, you don't feel emotionally attached to constantly moving the steering wheel when you drive; you consider this as a necessary course correction. It can be the same with our lives. Circumstances are constantly changing, requiring us to change the way we handle different situations.

Exercise:

Think of an event in your life for which you did not accept responsibility or felt like you were a victim. Ask yourself what you believed about that situation. What would you have to believe in order to change that situation? Maybe you would have to believe you deserve more than what you're getting. Maybe you'd have to believe it would be easy to get whatever it is that you want. Develop a strategy for changing your mental values and beliefs. Take action to implement the strategy.

Affirmation:

I claim my spiritual power to create everything I want in my life by accepting responsibility for it, and I commit to create a life that is exactly what I want it to be.

A Rose Garden

Focus on the Important Things

"The greatest use of life is to spend it for something that will outlast it."
William James

Most of our lives are extremely full, and there are more things to do than there is time to do them. Consequently, we end up being driven by the urgent things in life, like grocery shopping, taking the kids back and forth to school or practice, household chores, homework, etc. These are things that need to be done, but because they aren't scheduled, they eat up all of our time, and there is no time to do the things that are really important to us.

When I speak about stress, I usually ask my audiences what they think causes it. The most common answer I hear is "not enough time." I also ask if any of them have ever received a terminal diagnosis. Almost always, someone has. I ask those people what difference it made in their lives. They usually say it was the best thing that ever happened to them. "It taught me what was important!" they'll say. Can we learn what is really important in our lives without having to receive a terminal diagnosis?

Do you have a list of the top three, five or ten things in your life that are the most important to you? What are they? Religion, family, health, career, having fun, being creative, learning, growing? In order for you to be able to do the things that are important, you must learn to prioritize— that is, scheduling things that are important to you and not allowing the urgent tasks to consume all of your time.

This sounds easy, but some of us find it nearly impossible to say no when someone asks us to do something. We are people pleasers, or we don't want to hurt someone's feelings, or we don't want to get into a disagreement or feel like a victim.

If you don't commit your energy and intention to the important things, the urgent things will run your life! If today were the last day of your life, you'd resent not being able to spend more time doing the things that were truly important to you. Do you have enough self-esteem to do what's important to you?

Exercise:

Make a list of the ten most important things in your life. Put this list in order of importance. How much time are you spending on each one of these areas on a weekly, monthly or annual basis? Take the top three areas of importance in your life and develop an action plan for committing the time, money and energy necessary for you to feel fulfilled in these areas. Tape your action plan to your bathroom mirror, and read the plan ten times every day. When you focus your energy and intention on doing the things that are truly important to you, they will happen.

Affirmation:

My life is committed to doing the things that are important to me.

A Rose Garden

Be All That You Can Be

"For life is the mirror of king and slave. 'Tis just what we are and do; then give to the world the best you have and the best will come back to you." Madeline Bridges

We are all giants, but most of us believe that we are dwarfs. We have tremendous skills, gifts, talents and abilities but have been taught to believe in our limitations instead. Henry Ford said, "Whether you think you can or think you can't, you're right." To be all that you can be, you must believe that you can. We're all unique. Our challenge, then, is to become who we are capable of being.

Have you heard the story about the eagle that was raised by a chicken in a hen yard? He was watching an adult eagle flying majestically overhead, and he and his siblings were longing to be eagles. But lo and behold, he was an eagle, and he didn't know it! What do you long to be that you may already be?

Let's take a look at some of the things that block us from becoming all that we can be. Perhaps we're intimidated by a parent, teacher or other authority figure that talks down to us, bullies us or intimidates us. This teaches us that we are less than adequate, which causes us to perform at much lower levels than we are capable. The effect is that we become less than we can be. It's a tragic waste of talent when we compromise our lives and our gifts because we're afraid of someone else's opinion of us. In order to be all that you can be, you must first believe in yourself, and then you must be the source of your validation. You cannot give your power to others by allowing them to establish your value in your mind.

I've always loved Terry Cole Whittaker's book *What You Think of Me Is None of My Business*. What a great title! How would your beliefs about yourself change if you adapted the attitude that what other people thought of you was none of your business? Hopefully, you would do what you believed was best for you. You would have much more confidence to reach out and try new and different things, because you gave people permission to think whatever they wanted to think of you. Your primary mission in life would be to make a significant, positive contribution to the world based on what was best for humankind, not what people thought of you.

Our tribe called "society" is going to try to get you to think, behave and live according to the norms and morals it has established. If you fall outside of the established norms if you're too creative or too inventive, if you're going faster than the rest of the tribe, the tribe will try to slow you down. The way they do this is by ostracizing you or, in extreme cases, executing you. The tribe tries to get everyone to live within the defined norms. Our challenge is not to succumb to those rules and mores but to be ourselves and become all that we can be.

Accept the premise that we are spiritual beings and that our physical bodies are not who we are. This belief enables us to focus and have the strength and the determination to be the spiritual beings that we are. It allows us to bring that level of awareness and divinity into our physical being. We now can become all that we can be without regard for how other people react or think. Be adventurous, be bold, be brave, and allow other people to express their beings in whatever way they choose, just as long as it doesn't harm you.

Now is the time to reevaluate the beliefs you follow that prohibit you from being all that you can be. Reach up, reach out and smash through limits that you never thought you could overcome.

A Rose Garden

Exercise:

Think of an area of your life where you have felt limited. What causes you to be limited in that area? What beliefs do you have that no longer serve you? What beliefs would you have to have in order to excel in that area? Set your goal as an intention, and be very clear what that intention is. Send it out into the universe. Know that because of the intensity of your intention and the focus you have, you will perform at the highest level you can.

Affirmation:

I am grateful for all the gifts that have been bestowed upon me by my creator. I promise to use all these gifts to their fullest ability.

Take Life One Step at a Time

"Life is a series of steps. Things are done gradually. Once in a while there is a giant step, but most of the time we are taking small, seemingly insignificant steps on the stairway of life." Ralph Ransom

Once when I was looking for a job, I was asked to memorize a thirteen-minute segment on audiotape and come in for an audition. I didn't want to do that, because I didn't want to work for that company. However, I was advised to go through each step of the interview, so I memorized the tape and went to the audition. I wasn't called back, but what I got out of that experience was the new belief that I could memorize. On my next interview I had a thirty-page script to memorize. I did it and got the job. Had I not taken the step of memorizing the thirteen-minute segment, I wouldn't have even tried to tackle the thirty-page script. I also learned that I could present a script and still inject my personality into it. This happened because I was willing to take the next step.

In this instance, my belief was that the outcome of getting the first job was the reason for going through the process. But it wasn't. The reason was to teach me that I could give a good presentation using memorized material.

Be willing to take the next step without knowing what the outcome will be. Always ask, "What is there to learn from this?" Trust the process. I believe progress is measured in lifetimes, not days, weeks, months or years.

When you accept the concept that the purpose of life is to learn lessons, the only way you can learn is to take action. When you get into a situation, it is vital to release your attachment to the outcome.

A Rose Garden

We tend to treat our perceived conclusion as if it were the only possible outcome. Remember to trust the process and release the need to control the outcome. As you take each step, ask yourself, "What is this in my life to teach me?"

Exercise:

Dick Sykes, a former boss, once told me the only way to eat an elephant is one bite at a time. This applies to every project we undertake in our life. Do it one step at a time. Break down a big task into bite sized pieces. For example, let's say you would like to lose forty pounds:

1. Set the goal—in this case, to lose forty pounds.
2. Do research about the kind of eating that you can incorporate into your life style.
3. Break the weight-loss goal down from forty pounds to two pounds per week. That's twenty weeks or about five months.
4. Set a start date.
5. Allow an extra month to lose the weight.
6. Don't be concerned about what the scale says.
7. Set a short-term goal of losing five pounds.
8. Set seven more goals of losing five pounds.

You have now broken a huge task down into small steps that are much easier to obtain.

Affirmation:

I savor every step in my life.

It's Not What Happens to You That Matters, It's What You Do About It

"I have given everything I see...all the meaning it has for me."
(*A Course in Miracles*, Workbook p. 4 1st edition p. 4 2nd edition)

Tragic things happen to everyone. Many would call these people victims, but those who accept the victim label give their power to tragic events. By believing that you are powerless, you lose the opportunity to learn from the event. You may not have control over it, but you have the power to decide how you will respond to it.

My friend W. Mitchell says he has experienced two major bumps on the road of life. First, he was hit by a laundry truck while riding his motorcycle. The collision ignited his gas tank, which gave him third degree burns over eighty percent of his body. The second bump happened when he was flying an airplane that was improperly deiced. When the plane crashed, he tried to get out if it, but he couldn't, because his spine had been severed.

Rather than feel sorry for himself the rest of his life and see himself as someone to be pitied, he became a professional speaker. He teaches people how to overcome obstacles to get the life of their dreams, and he receives a five-figure income every time he speaks. His motto is "It's not what happens to you that matters, it is what you do about it."

I knew a man who was in an automobile accident, at the age of 23, that left him a quadriplegic. After struggling to regain some mobility, he decided to get a job as a salesman. He sounded impressive over the phone, but when he arrived at the interview in a wheelchair, his prospective employers were shocked and didn't give Art the job. He continued to pursue his dream and became a motivational speaker,

A Rose Garden

receiving over $10,000 per program and conducting 180 programs a year. He also got married and had two children.

How do you handle adversity in your life? In order to maximize the lessons from these events, it's important to take a look at how we perceive them. When we perceive an event as a tragedy, we typically respond in a negative fashion. One of the best ways to create power in our lives is to ask better questions. In both of the stories I just shared, the powerful question was, "How can I turn this event into an advantage?" My favorite quote from A Course in Miracles is, "What could you not accept if you but knew everything that happens, past, present and to come, is gently planned by one whose only purpose is your good?" (Workbook, p.247 1st edition p. 255 2nd editon) In other words, what couldn't you accept if you knew everything that happened in your life was a gift from God?

When something negative happens in your life, you may want to talk to God. You may say, "God, this really doesn't look like a gift. It doesn't smell like a gift. It doesn't taste like a gift. It really looks terrible. But because I know how much your love me and I absolutely know that this is a gift from you to me, I will try to find the gift in this event." Ask yourself, "Where is the gift?" until you get an answer that gives you a sense of peace. This means that the Spirit has spoken.

Exercise:

When you are in an unpleasant situation, ask yourself where the gift is until you receive the answer. Look for the answer on television or the radio, in something you read or something someone says to you, or in your prayers and meditation. Your answer won't necessarily come to you as a sentence in your mind.

Affirmation:

I'm thrilled that God is my partner, and I trust that all the events that happen to me are gifts from Him. With His assistance, I will find the gift in every event in my life and will be grateful for it.

A Rose Garden

Ease and Dis-Ease

"Whenever we are ill, we need to look around to see who it is that we need to forgive." Louise Hay

In Louise Hay's book *You Can Heal Your Life*, the author refers to disease as "dis-ease." Her point of view is that we create the things that happen to us. We create with our thoughts. We continue to have the same thoughts for a long period of time, thereby converting repetitive thoughts into beliefs. Holding onto unhealthy beliefs eventually converts those beliefs from a mental state into a physical state. That physical state is dis-ease.

Most people believe they are the victims of dis-ease. Very few, however, believe they have the power to create that dis-ease, and they say they would never do that such a thing to themselves. If we are honest, however, we know that we sabotage ourselves all the time. If we create strong beliefs about not being good enough, it can manifest itself in a dis-ease. The irony here is that we would rather believe we are victims than accept the fact that we have power we didn't know we had. Now that we know we have it, we can create the things we want in our lives rather than the things we don't want.

Assume for a minute that you have the power to create dis-ease. Until now, you didn't know you could create it, so you focused on the negative things in your life and thus created what you didn't want. Now that you know you can create dis-ease, you need to shift your focus from the things you don't want to the things you do want. This requires that you become aware of your thoughts. When you find yourself dwelling on negativity, you must immediately switch your thoughts to what you want.

Your mind is a magnet. It will bring to you whatever it focuses on consistently. That is the job of your subconscious mind—to make whatever you believe come true. Furthermore, it can't distinguish between fact and fiction. The affirmations at the end of every chapter in this book are there to reinforce the messages to your subconscious mind.

What thoughts do you have that could possibly create dis-ease? Hay's book contains a chart of diseases along with the beliefs that cause them. She says that people who have cancer have stuffed their anger for years. This repressed anger begins to manifest itself physically and starts destroying the body.

Dig deep for the answers here, because your ego is not going to make it easy for you to find the answers. This will require thought and meditation. If you have cancer, ask yourself, "What am I angry about?" Be honest with yourself.

Once you have looked closely at your own state of dis-ease, be it mild or serious. ask yourself how you might begin to create more ease in your life.

Exercise:

Go to your favorite place in the world, either physically or in your mind. Sit there and relax. Go there at a time where you know you won't be disturbed. Ask yourself, your guide, your angel, God or whomever you believe in as a higher power, "What belief created this disease?" What do your beliefs need to be in order to heal this disease? What is this disease meant to teach you?

Affirmation:

I know the lessons that disease is there to teach me, and I am committed to learning the lessons without disease.

A Rose Garden

Would You Rather Be Right or Happy?

"Happiness? That's nothing more than good health and a poor memory." Albert Schweitzer

It is more important to be happy than to be right. This has been one of my major life lessons. At one time I believed all that mattered was being right. When I worked as an assistant hospital administrator, my boss said to me one day, "Jim, I know what's going to be written on your tombstone: 'He was always right.'" I thought that was awesome! What a tremendous compliment to get from the administrator! I had no idea that he was counseling me. I had no idea how difficult or impossible it was to work with someone who thinks he's always right.

My wife and I, like a lot of couples, compete about being right. As I continue to learn this lesson, I am able to let go of the need to be right more often. The reality is that one or two weeks from now, you're not even going to remember whatever issue you had to be right about, let alone whether you were right or not. The difficulty is that when you engage with another human being in needing to be right, one person has to be right and the other has to be wrong. When one is right and one is wrong, that's a win-lose situation. All win-lose situations translate to lose-lose. Unless the situation is win-win, it's lose-lose. Life is too short to create losing situations for ourselves.

What's truly important in life is being happy. And what easier way to be happy than to make other people happy? If I make you feel good about who you are, if I make you feel good about being with me, if I make you feel important, revered, respected and admired, you're going to be happy. And guess what: You're going to love to be with me!

What are some of the things we say that indicate we need to be right? We frequently use phrases like, "No, it's this way," "I don't see it that way" or "Really, this is what it is." How often do you correct someone about something that really is incidental? It makes no difference whether you paid $4.99 or $4.95 for something. What's driving you is the need, the compulsion to be right. Release your need to be right. Embrace your desire to be happy, and your whole attitude about life will change.

Exercise:

Identify one person in your life with whom you feel most strongly the need to be right. Identify one person in your life with whom you don't feel the need to be right—all you want is to be with that person and be happy. What do you believe about that person? Once you've identified that belief, adopt it when you are with the person with whom you need to be right. It will have an amazing impact on your relationship. Wait until you see how they change because your attitude about them has changed.

Affirmation:

I am committed to a life of happiness. I release the need to be right.

A Rose Garden

Be Flexible

"Minds are like parachutes; they work best when they are open."
Lord Thomas Dewar

The more rigid we are in our views and beliefs about how life works, the more pain we experience. The value of being flexible is that you're ready for any assignment. Remember that we're here to learn lessons and that each day, new assignments may come along. If you're rigid, you'll resist those assignments, you'll be angry and hostile, you will withdraw, and you'll miss the opportunities. Every event in life has a certain useful existence. When that time is over—whether it lasts a few seconds or an entire lifetime—it's time to move on to the next step.

Another way to be flexible is to have a carefree attitude, no matter what happens. "I'm not going to resist anything. I may need to refocus in order to gain a new prospective on it, and I'm willing to do that." When you feel yourself becoming rigid, that's a message that you're resisting. One of the key elements to a successful life is to identify what we're resisting. When you do, back off, refocus, change your perception about what's going on, and find a way to embrace the new concept or lifestyle that has been thrust upon you.

In order to learn lessons, it is important to be open and receptive to the different ways you can learn. Let go of the past and be open to attracting new opportunities, new challenges and new ways to learn and grow. Life works in an absolutely perfectly timed way. When you are ready to learn the lesson, it will be presented. As the Buddhist proverb says, when the student is ready, the teacher appears. One has to be willing to let go.

I once went through a training program where one of our

challenges was to climb a sixty-two-foot pole and then jump out and catch a trapeze ten feet away. I noticed that the people who jumped to catch the trapeze with their arms held straight out never were able to hold on. The reason was that they did not have enough strength to absorb the change in direction of the energy. It all had to be absorbed in their fingers, and they didn't have the strength to do that. However, the people who caught the trapeze with their arms bent were able to hold on to the trapeze. The successful people flexed their arms and were able to absorb the change.

Exercise:

Identify the three areas of your life where you consider yourself to be the most flexible. Write down the beliefs you have about those areas. Apply those beliefs to the area of your life where you tend to be the most rigid. Keep a journal and record how these beliefs open up new opportunities in the area in which you were most rigid.

Affirmation:

I am mentally, spiritually and physically flexible and embrace my flexibility as a sign of my openness to receive God's love into my life.

A Rose Garden

Your Parents Couldn't Teach You Skills They Didn't Have

"Give a man a fish and he will eat for a day. Teach a man to fish and he will eat for the rest of his life." Chinese proverb

Could you teach me to speak Chinese? No? Why not? Probably because you don't speak Chinese. Let's apply that same thinking to your parents. If they didn't have a good sense of self, how could they have taught you to have a good sense of self? They couldn't teach you a skill they didn't have.

Releasing your parents of blame allows you the freedom to get on with your life. They did the best they could do with the resources they had available to them at the time. It's my point of view that we choose our parents, because they are the best teachers of many of the lessons we came here to learn! Consequently, we should be grateful to them for teaching us what they did. They taught us to be who we are.

I have two suggestions: First, forgive your parents for not giving you the things you think they should have. Second, accept responsibility for the fact that you chose them as your parents and that they were incredible teachers. I understand that maybe a lot of the things they taught you may have been negative but these experiences make you the person you are today. However, if you created a belief to get you through a very difficult situation when you were a child, it may be time to review that belief and decide if it serves you today. If not, create a belief today that serves you in you present life.

Oftentimes very negative situations become our greatest teachers and lessons. It often takes time to gain that perspective. Remember the poem "Footprints in the Sand" by Mary Stevenson? In the poem, a person dreams of walking on the beach with God. She imagined many scenes of her life, and noticed two sets of footprints in some scenes, and only one set in others, and those were at the most difficult times of her life. She challenged God, saying, "You promised me Lord, that if I would follow you, you would walk with me always." God replied, " The years when you have seen only one set of footprints, my child, is when I carried you." I invite you to take a moment and wrap your arms around God's neck and wrap your legs around God's waist and let God carry you through the difficult times of your life.

What are some of the things that you wish your parents had given you? Because they weren't able to give them to you does not mean that you cannot give them to yourself. It's never too late. The past is the past, and it only exists in your mind. You have to decide what you want for yourself and your future. Believe that you're worth it, and then do the things that need to be done in order to get them.

Exercise:

Make a list of the skills you wish you had received from your parents. Pick the three skills that are the most important for you to have. Develop an action plan for how you're going to develop that quality.

Affirmation:

I commit to taking the action necessary to develop the skills and talents that I now consider to be vital to a happy and successful life.

A Rose Garden

Leave a Lasting Legacy

"At birth we come; at death we go, leaving nothing." Chinese proverb

For all of recorded history, man has asked the question, "Why am I here? What is the purpose of my life?" I believe that one of the purposes of life is to create a lasting legacy. How is the world a better place because we lived here? What do we mean to others? How do we make a difference in their lives? It's important to understand that our words and actions create our reputation.

How do you want people to remember you? Once you know how you want to be remembered you can start to create, or continue creating, your legacy. To be remembered the way you want will require that you consistently express certain characteristics. If you want your legacy to be " she was a great mom", then you will want to determine what you believe the characteristics of a great mom are. You may even want to keep that list with you. Let that be your North Star. After all, this is how you want to define your life. It is an incredible opportunity to create the kind of life you want.

When you live your life consciously, creating a lasting legacy, two things will happen: You will create an awesome legacy, and your life will be incredibly fulfilling because you are living as your true self.

Exercise:

Fast-forward to your memorial service and imagine what people would say about you if they were completely honest. Now decide what you want them to say about you. Complete the plan for how you are going to create your lasting legacy and bring it to life. You will be creating an incredible life while you are in the process.

Affirmation:

My life is a living testament to my being a divine being in a physical body. I invite the divine presence of my creator to work in and through me every moment of my life.

A Rose Garden

Part 3

Core Principles on Which to Build Your Life

A Rose Garden

You Co-Create Your Universe

"Whether you think you can or you think you can't, you are right."
Henry Ford

You and the universe are partners. The universe is here to give you all you want for yourself and everyone else. You just need to identify what you want. You do that through your beliefs and actions. You must stand up for yourself and say, "I deserve this." Do that repeatedly and you will create the energy needed to manifest your desires. You will become the architect that designs your dream life.

However, you're not the general contractor; the universe is. Release to the universe a general plan rather than one that has too many specifics. Don't say, "I want the house at 123 Elm Street," but on the other hand, don't just say, "I want a million dollars." There is the story of the taxi driver who asked for a million dollars, but he didn't specify how it should come to him. He was injured in an auto accident that left him a quadriplegic. He won $1.5 million from the lawsuit. Then there's the former co-worker of mine who prayed to have a baby. She did, but the father wasn't there to help her raise it. You have to be specific in terms of how you want things to happen, but if you get too specific, the dream becomes too restrictive for the universe to create.

The universe is generous. I invite you to take that fact at face value, and to bring that mentality to the table when I ask you what you want for yourself. What is your ideal life? What would a perfect day look and feel like for you? There are no rules. Once you conceive it, you must believe it, and then release it to the universe to create it or something better.

You are in a sacred partnership with the universe, and each partner has a responsibility. Your partner cannot do anything until you fulfill your responsibility, which is simply to tell it what you want. Give God the assignment and allow your partner to complete the assignment without any doubting or nagging on your part.

Exercise:

Create a thought about something you want in life. Develop the thought in great detail. If you want a new home, visualize what it looks like. See yourself moving happily around the house. Hold the thought in your mind as if it already exists. Develop an affirmation about your desire: "I live happily in my new home and can easily afford it." Indicate that you want this home or one that's even better. Release your dream to be created. Know that it will come to you.

Affirmation:

I trust in the partnership I have with the universe to create everything that I tell it I want. The universe and I co-create my life.

A Rose Garden

The Power of Thoughts

"The power of thought, the magic of the mind."
George Gordon Byron

Science teaches us that all of life is energy moving at different speeds. Dense energy moves very slowly, like in a rock or a mountain. There are also things that vibrate at higher speeds, beyond our ability to see and hear them. For example, if you look at the spectrum of light, there are certain lights and colors that we can see, but when light vibrates at higher rates, we are no longer able to see it.

Likewise, our thoughts vibrate at different energies. Negative thoughts have a heavy, dense vibration. Light, happy and ecstatic thoughts vibrate at higher levels and can change the chemical composition of our bodies, too. Because our thoughts vibrate at different levels, they are able to create matter.

According to Tom G. Stevens, PhD in his book *You Can Choose To Be Happy: "Rise Above" Anger, Anxiety, and Depression*, we have about 60,000 thoughts every day. Unfortunately, most of those thoughts are the same day in and day out. If you kept a detailed log of what was going on in your life today, I could look back a year from now and see how your thoughts helped create what happened in the following year. Our thoughts are that accurate in predicting and creating the future.

When things in our lives aren't working out, we tend to dwell on it, not realizing that by maintaining those thoughts we are creating a future that we don't want. We need to focus our thoughts on how we want our lives to be, not on how they are. Thoughts create, so you must now decide what future you want to create. This is why you cannot allow negative thoughts to continue to hold a place in your life.

Your challenge is to find a way to identify when you're thinking negatively, stop it and refocus on what you would consider your ideal life. It is not necessary for you to know how something is going to come into your life. Hold strong to your convictions and you will create it. Give thanks and carry on with the absolute knowledge that it has been created. Let me say that again: *It has been created.* The only thing you don't know is when it will be delivered. This requires trust. Trust the laws of life that say you are the co-creator of your future.

Exercise:

For the next week, keep a log of your negative thoughts. Whenever you are consciously aware of having a negative thought, interrupt it and replace it with a positive vision of your future. This vision does not have to include the procedure for how it will be completed. That's not your responsibility. Your responsibility is to create the concept. The universe will go though the practical steps of how to materialize the concept you've created.

Affirmation:

The most powerful tool to create in my life is my thoughts. I use my thoughts to create a world that is for my highest good and for the highest good of all concerned.

A Rose Garden

Life Will Change

"Life is the continual adjustment of external relations."
Herbert Spencer

In my speaking career, I am asked to speak more about change than any other subject. I talk about overcoming the fear of change. I believe that no matter what our level of success, we get comfortable with where we are, and we fear change. We're afraid of change, because we operate at a certain level of expertise. When something changes, like a computer system, a relationship or a job, we are uncomfortable with the situation until we adjust to the change.

Remember how you felt during a time when you were learning something, and appreciate the level of confidence and expertise you have with it now. An important factor in adjusting to change is being willing to live with the discomfort of temporarily operating at a lower level. It's important that we are willing to experience that discomfort. Don't try to run away from it, hide it or deny it. Just be there with it, and allow it to motivate you to move ahead to a level of confidence at which you know you're capable of functioning.

The most certain fact of life is that life is going to change. If you know that your life is going to change, stop trying to avoid the inevitable. Absolutely every aspect of your life will change at least once during your life—probably many times. Accept that change is as basic as breathing. Don't fight it and stop trying to go back. Doors are closing behind you all the time; don't keep banging on them, trying to get them open. When one door closes, move on to the next one.

Imagine how your life would change if every time something happened you said, "Okay, what's next? Gee, that's neat. I got fired. I didn't like that job anyway." Cultivate the "what's next" attitude instead of trying to hold on or being fearful and angry.

See change as the vehicle that gets you through life. If you have a beat-up '67 Volkswagen, it might not start all the time, it might have bumps and dents, and it might barely make it from one place to the other. Or you could have a sleek new sports car as the vehicle that gets you though life.

My point of view is that life is about learning lessons. In order for us to learn our lessons, every aspect of life has to change. Once we've learned those lessons, we're different. Therefore, our approach to life is different. How we perceive things is different, and consequently, how other people perceive us changes. Some of the changes in life are subtle; some are enormous. The reality is that we have everything it takes to meet the challenge of change, no matter how big that change is. Embrace change. Get excited about the changes that are happening in your life. Know that it means that you are going to grow and become a fuller person.

Exercise:

Write down your beliefs about the area of your life that is easiest to change. Do the same for the area of your life that is the most difficult to change. Now take the beliefs you have about the area of your life where it's easiest for you to change and apply them to the area of your life that is most difficult for you to change.

Affirmation:

I embrace change as the highest form of love in life.

A Rose Garden

To Change the Outcomes in Your Life, You Must Change Your Actions

"I am not discouraged, because every wrong attempt discarded is another step forward." Thomas A. Edison

Every time we do something, the result is either an outcome we want or one that we don't want. The definition of insanity that I like best is "doing the same thing over and over again and expecting a different result."

If we were in a scientific laboratory and got undesirable results, we would never duplicate the experiment. We would change at least one element of it, knowing that it could possibly change the outcome. Our procedure would systematically change until we got the desired outcome. When we did so, we would duplicate the procedure every time.

My wife is very hard-working, and she rarely leaves work on time. When I'm feeling resentful, as I occassionally do, that her dedication to the job is eating into our time together at home, the appropriate action would be to tell her how happy I am to see her and ask her if there is anything I could do to make her comfortable. In other words, I could do things that would make her more eager to come home and be with me. Instead, I give her a hard time for coming home late. I don't reinforce the behavior I want; I make the mistake of reinforcing the behavior I *don't* want. She comes home late and I complain; therefore, I imagine I'm not giving her much incentive to come home earlier.

When you want someone's behavior to change, reinforce the behaviors you want. Sometimes I don't call my mother for a month or two. When I do call her, she reminds me that I haven't called in a long time, which feels to me like a complaint. What she doesn't realize is that a more positive approach—complimenting me when I do call—would likely give me more incentive to call more often.

What are some examples in your life where you can clearly see how you need to behave in order to get the outcomes you want? What changes do you have to make to get the results you want?

Exercise:

Identify something irritating that someone close to you does. What would you like him to do instead? What behaviors would you have to change in order to get him to do what you want? Take that action. Did the action result in the desired outcome? If you don't get the outcome you want, change your behavior until you do.

Affirmation:

I commit to changing the actions in my life in order to get the outcomes that will enable me to live my dream life.

A Rose Garden

Reprogram Your Subconscious Mind

"The real man lies in the depths of the subconscious." H.L. Menken

The subconscious mind is an absolute slave. It does exactly what you tell it to do. It doesn't know the difference between the truth and a lie, between what's really going on in your life and what you program it to do. Its job is to take the thoughts that you consistently have and make them into a reality. Effectively, what we're doing is programming our subconscious minds. The subconscious mind does not question the information that it receives from the conscious mind; it just implements it. If you say to yourself, "I'm stupid," the subconscious mind assumes this is the truth and creates events in your life to make you right.

Let's say that the captain of a ship is the conscious mind, while the navigator who sets the course for the ship is the subconscious mind. The captain can tell the navigator what coordinates he wants and what speed he wants the ship to go. The navigator's sole responsibility is to carry out the captain's orders and set the ship to go at that speed. The captain could be telling him to head straight into the side of a mountain at full speed, but the navigator does not question those orders.

Similarly, the course of your life is based on how your conscious mind has programmed your subconscious mind. If you would like to change your life, you have to change the instructions you give your subconscious mind. You have to control your thoughts. In the Bible, there's a verse that says that we need to be the gatekeepers of our minds. I think that's true. We have to guard the thoughts we have, because they have the power to create a life that we're not even aware we're creating. Now that you're aware of it, your responsibility is to guard your thoughts diligently and not program your subconscious mind to create a life that you don't want.

When you begin the process of reprogramming, your subconscious will tell you, "You've got to be kidding! You're telling me you want to be thin when all your life you've been heavy?" It will challenge you. However, you have to say, "Yes, that's what I want. I want to be thin. Change things so that I am thin."

And you can't have contradictory thoughts. You can't go out to dinner, eat a rich dessert and say, "Oh my God, I shouldn't have had this, because it will make me fatter." This is an expression of your subconscious beliefs, which it will continue to give you what you have always had—a weight problem.

Exercise:

Define the area of your life you want to change most. Make a list of the things that are sabotaging you. If you're overweight, list the foods you eat that keep you heavy, the time of day you eat, your age, your metabolism. All of those are thoughts that are causing you to program your subconscious mind to ensure that you stay heavy. Write down what you want instead. Write down all the thoughts and beliefs that you would have to have in order for this to become a reality. Develop a mantra from these beliefs, e.g., "I am thin, I am wealthy, I am an extraordinary example of health," etc. Repeat this affirmation a minimum of a 100 times a day for thirty days.

Affirmation:

I am _____ (Fill in the blank with whatever you desire for your life.)

A Rose Garden

Abundance

"There is nothing on earth you cannot have—once you have mentally accepted the fact that you can have it." Robert Collier

We live in a world of unlimited abundance. There is an abundance of wealth, natural resources, love—anything we can imagine. However, we believe that we live in a world of scarcity, and therefore, we have created a world of scarcity. Because we believe that there isn't enough, we fear there won't be enough for us and that other people will take what we have. We see these people as our enemies, and they see us as their enemies.

In Susan Jeffers's book *Feel the Fear and Do It Anyway*, the author says that we should feel the fear of not having enough money or food, not being able to pay bills and giving of ourselves at the risk of being rejected. But now also imagine what it feels like to have the absolute knowledge that there is an infinite abundance of everything! Decide which way you would rather feel, because you can create your reality! This requires letting go of limiting beliefs. Are those limiting beliefs worth the price you are paying for them?

When we hold on to things, we stop the flow of abundance in life, and when we stop the flow, we create the fear. Recessions and depressions occur when the flow of the money is slowed down and people get scared. People believe there isn't enough to go around, so they stop buying cars, houses, washing machines, etc. When companies have lower sales, they lay people off. Those people don't have the purchasing power to purchase other things, which means that other people will lose their jobs, and the cycle continues.

Do not allow fear to govern your life. Reach out and give in every area in your life, knowing that it will come back. You'll never know where, how or when it will come back, but be absolutely assured that whatever you give will come back. Zig Ziglar believes that we will get everything we want in life when we help enough people get everything they want. So share your time, talent and money. Share your gifts and your knowledge, because by sharing them, they will increase in an exponential fashion.

We're all here together, and everything we have should be shared so we can grow collectively as a people and find our way back to our source, to our creator, together. Give of yourself with the vision of contributing to the betterment of society and you will benefit from a society that functions at a higher level. If all of us had the goal in our lives of raising the consciousness of all the lives we touch, the world would be an absolutely magnificent place in which to live.

Exercise:

Identify one area of your life you would like to share with other people. How can you share the gifts that have been given to you? Develop a plan to expand your vision of what sharing means and how it will impact your life and the lives of everyone you touch. All of us have thrown a stone into a pond of water and watched the ripples spread outward. Throw your stone into the pond and watch how sharing with other people can have a ripple effect on the entire world.

Affirmation:

I live in a world overflowing with abundance. Everything I have I share with everyone who touches my life.

A Rose Garden

The Importance of Values

A musician must make music, an artist must paint, a poet must write, if he is to be ultimately at peace with himself." Abraham Maslow

Tony Robbins has had a great influence on me over the years. His books, lectures, and ideas have become so much a part of the way I think I can scarcely remember where I heard what. But his lessons, and in particular what he has taught me about values, are certainly reflected in my thinking here, and I'm indebted to him for his inspiration.

There are two kinds of values— those we should move toward (love, adventure, acceptance, challenge) and those we should move away from (fear, frustration, anger, hostility, embarrassment). People are more generally motivated to move away from negative values. If one of your negative values is avoiding conflict, you are more motivated to avoid conflict than to move through the conflict into peace.

We all have values that govern our lives, yet we don't know what they are or how we prioritize them. For example, if two people are in a relationship in which one values security and the other values adventure, there is a high probability of problems arising in the relationship. Or let's say that two people both value honesty; however, one person believes in being totally honest at the expense of tact and sensitivity, while the other person is honest in a loving way. Both have the same value, but each defines it differently.

The values you have now aren't necessarily the ones you'll have for the rest of your life. But if you are who you want to be, if your life is going the way you want it to go, then you can maintain the values you have and keep the same definition. Either way, it's critical to know your values; how you define them determines the quality of your life and the relationships you have with other people. Most people never define their values, let alone the values of their mates.

If you want to change your life, the first thing you have to know is what kind of life you want. Imagine it in detail and then determine what kinds of values are needed in order to have that kind of life. Finally, you need to define those values. How do you know when you're being loved? How do you know when you're a success? How do you know when you're being compassionate?

Exercise:

Make a list of your top twenty-five values and then prioritize them. Define your top ten values. If love is one of your top values, how do you know when you are being loved? Is it something that the person says to you? Is it something he or she does? Is it a feeling you have? Now determine what values you would have to have to live the life you want. Review this list every three to six months to determine if you want to change the values or the definitions.

Affirmation:

My divinity is expressed and experienced through the values with which I choose to live my life.

A Rose Garden

Honor the Beauty and the Differences in Others

"Believe the best about people, and if you are wrong, you have only erred on the side of love." Robert H. Schuller

If you think the world is corrupt, you will look for evidence to support your belief. And when you find it, you will say, "See? I told you so!" There's the story about the man who walks into a café and says to the waiter that he's thinking of moving to a new town and he's considering this one. He asks the waiter "What are the people like in this town?" The waiter says, "What are they like in the town you live in now?" "Oh, they're unfriendly, small-minded, not very creative or worldly," the visitor says. The waiter says, "That's what the people are like in this town." Later, another man steps into the same café, says he's thinking of moving to town, and asks the waiter the same question, "What are the people like in this town?" The waiter replies, "What are the people like in the town where you live now?" The visitor says, "They're wonderful! Neighborly, involved—very creative, intelligent people." The waiter replied, "That's what the people are like in this town." In other words, you will find whatever you look for.

What would your ideal world be like? Look for those qualities in everyone you see and meet. Look for the beauty in everyone you meet; I guarantee that you will find it, and when you do, honor it. It may come across differently than the way you express the same quality, but that's because we are all different. Honor those differences. They are there to open your eyes to the possibilities.

When you go looking for the beauty in another person, pick one area you want to explore. Let's say you want to see other people express love. For the next week, whenever you meet somebody, ask, "How do you express love in your life?" You will be amazed at what you find.

The value of our differences is one of the most magnificent ways we have to teach each other the power of our uniqueness. We express our differences with everything from our religions and the colors of our skin to our careers and points of view. The most important thing you can do is honor the differences in other people. That is what makes them who they are. It doesn't matter what the outside wrapping looks like. What matters is on the inside. All you have to do is look for the beauty.

Exercise:

Think of three qualities that you want everyone in the world to express. Develop three questions that will enable you to look for these qualities in everyone you meet. For ten days, ask one of these questions whenever you meet someone; write down your observations. For the next ten days, ask another question and continue to write down your observations. Finally, ask your last question during the third ten-day period. At the end of each ten-day period review your findings. The results will change the way you see the world, and therefore, your world will change! I promise.

Affirmation:

I see and honor the beauty in everyone. I love to explore the differences in everyone I meet. We all have such different and magnificent ways to express our divinity.

A Rose Garden

Communication

"Don't use time or words carelessly. Neither can be retrieved."
H. Jackson Brown

We communicate every day of our lives, whether it's with our words, our tone or our body language. But how effectively are we communicating? I know from personal experience that I sometimes do a horrible job of communicating with my wife. And when she doesn't understand me, I blame her! I assume that she communicates the same way I do, even when I know that's not the case. That's where our communication problems begin. Meanwhile, if I have the attitude that she should learn to communicate to me the way that I want to be communicated with, it creates a lose-lose situation. I know how she wants to be communicated with, yet I get stubborn and want her to come to me first. Successful communication is the responsibility of the person doing the communicating. It's my responsibility to find words that have meaning to her.

A friend of mine, Jim Zinger, once told me, "You need to communicate not to be understood, but not to be misunderstood." How would your communication change if the reason you communicated was to be sure that you were not misunderstood? You would ask more questions, get more feedback and test to see if what you meant was what actually got communicated.

The first thing we do when we communicate is formulate a thought and send it from the brains to the mouth. However, we are able to think a lot faster then we're able to talk, so once we have a thought and send it to our mouth, we move on to the next thought. Thus, we don't always say what we intend to say, or the words we use do not mean the same to the person we're talking to as they do to us.

I experienced a great example of this once at a Tony Robbins seminar. It was a Friday night, and Tony said, "We're going to start at 10:00 a.m. tomorrow." Then he added, "What does that mean to you?" I thought, "What a stupid question. There's only one minute in the day that's called 10:00 a.m. What else could it possibly mean?"

One person raised her hand and gave the same definition as me. Someone else raised his hand and said it meant 10:05 a.m. Another person raised his hand and said it meant 10:15. This went on and on. It absolutely dumfounded me that there could be that many different meanings for something I knew only had one meaning. It's your responsibility to find out what meanings others attach to what you say. We have problems when we make assumptions that others attach the same interpretations to our statements that we do. That just isn't the case.

Another significant aspect of communication is our tone, or how we say the words. If you ask me how I am, I could say "fine" with no emotion or I could say it in such a way that lets you know I'm really angry. The same word said in a different way has two totally different meanings.

The last, and perhaps most significant, element of communication is body language. Again, we could say something one way, but our body language could totally change the meaning. You will want to practice all three areas of communication. The more aware we are of what we're doing, the more accurate we are.

Also, be conscious of other people's words, tone and body language. We tend to subconsciously interpret them without realizing it. One of my favorite sayings about communication is from Stephen Covey's book *The Seven Habits of Highly Effective People* (p. 237): "Seek first to

A Rose Garden

understand and then to be understood." Don't be afraid to ask a person, "What do you mean when you say that?" Ask gently, kindly and with patience. Each of us has a different communication style. (I won't be going into that here, but I recommend taking a class on the subject.) When we learn what the other person really means, we become more effective in our own communication.

Exercise:

With whom do you have the greatest difficulty communicating? With whom do you find it easiest to communicate? Write down all the traits of the person you find easiest to communicate with. Assign those traits to the person with whom you're having the most difficulty communicating. This will change your perception of the person, and your attitude about him or her will change. Then the way the two of you communicate will change.

Affirmation:

As a student of life, I look forward to every communication as a primary source of learning my life lessons.

Learn the Art of Listening

"Learn to listen. Opportunity sometimes knocks very softly."
H. Jackson Brown

As I mentioned in Part 2, my father-in-law always used to tell me that we have two ears and one mouth so we can listen twice as much as we talk. This is another life lesson I am trying to learn. We know what our attitudes, beliefs and convictions are, but we're not going to learn anything when we're talking. We will learn when we're listening to other people.

Listening is perhaps the most valuable skill we can develop. Listening means not only hearing the words and being able to repeat them but understanding the meaning behind the words. It means observing body language, making eye contact, listening for tone, probing and reading between the lines. You hear with your ears, but you listen with your ears, eyes, brain and heart.

Listening to people makes them feel appreciated and valued, but unfortunately, most people feel they're not listened to. One of the greatest gifts we can give others is to be completely attentive to them. Perhaps you have had experience being a good listener. Maybe you have had conversations in which you hardly said a word and the other person walked away thinking that you were a great person.

The first time I experienced that was before a Tony Robbins seminar. I walked up to him in the back of the room as he was preparing for his talk. Although there were 300 people walking around the room, he gave me his undivided attention. His eyes never moved from my eyes. He was there one-hundred-percent there for me.

A Rose Garden

Exercise:

Who is the best listener you know? The next time you speak with that person, pay attention to what she does that makes you know she's listening to you. What does she do with her eyes? What kinds of questions does she ask? Define those results. Pick two or three you consider most important. As you listen to others, add those skills to your tool box. As you become proficient at each one, go back to your list and add another one.

Affirmation:

I am a great listener.

Learn to Manage the Energies of Life

"Everything is energy in motion." Pir Vilayat Inayat Khan

Life is made up of all different kinds of energy. Have you ever walked into a room where everyone was yelling and cheering and you felt the energy in the room? You could literally feel the happiness and ecstasy. Conversely, we've all had the experience of walking into a room and feeling the heaviness in the air.

Energy also has an impact on our states of mind. It can either limit you or free you to do whatever you want. For example, the energy of anger is so intense that it easily draws us into it. We have to manage our energy so we exude positivism, not anger. If somebody is angry, we can react in anger or interpret the anger as a call for love and respond accordingly. At a minimum, we want to free ourselves of negative energy. If you suddenly get angry or upset at someone, walk away. If you get twenty-five feet away and don't feel that way anymore, you know it was probably the other person's anger that you were picking up on. If you still feel it, then you know it's your anger.

When I first had the idea for this book, an author friend sent me an e-mail telling me all the things that I would need to do to make it a great book. Honestly, I was a little intimidated. My initial reaction was that writing this book was a terrible idea. I wrote him back, telling him that what I really needed was his support, guidance and approval. He said he didn't intend to be disapproving but thought he was just giving me suggestions for how to make the book more marketable. My interpretation of what he said dictated my response.

We choose to be negative or depressed. When we make that choice, we give our power up to our perceptions of events. But we are

A Rose Garden

free to give them a different meaning and reclaim our power. Managing energy in your life requires a conscious effort and it takes practice.

Let's look at some ways to better manage our energy. Tony Robbins suggests that when you're depressed, you should change your physiology. Stand up, speak loudly and strongly, hold your head up high, thrust your arms into the air and smile. Put your book down and try this! See if you can feel depressed throwing your shoulders back, thrusting your arms into the air, smiling and shouting "Life is awesome!" When you did those things, the cells in your body changed. They actually moved faster.

Now find ways to renew your energy and lift your spirits every day to heighten your spirituality. Be aware of all of your energies— positive, neutral and negative. Develop a plan for what you're going to do to overcome dense, negative energy the next time you detect it. Be one who is going to lift other people's energy, who is going to make their lives seem better and lighter. We all make a difference every day. The question isn't whether we will make a difference but whether that difference will be positive or negative.

Exercise:

For the next week, practice identifying different kinds of energy. Give them names and jot them down in a notebook. It could be depression, anger, hostility, ecstasy, joy, etc. Rank them on a scale from one to five, with one being the lowest and five being the highest. At the end of the week, review your notes and determine the predominant kind of energy in the people with whom you came into contact. Decide what you have to do physically and mentally to change that energy. Maybe you should walk away from it, sever the relationship or say something to change the mindset. Instead of asking people how they are, ask, "What is the best thing that has happened to you today?" Or "Tell me who you are most grateful to have in your life?" Play around with the questions you ask people to change that energy. Notice how this shifts your energy as well.

Affirmation:

I ride the waves of life's high energy.

A Rose Garden

The Cost of Holding a Grudge

"To err is human, to forgive divine." Alexander Pope

I'm sure that at sometime in your life, you have held a grudge against another person. But do you realize the physical, mental and emotional price you pay to hold a grudge? First of all, you have to carry it with you twenty-four hours a day, seven days a week for as long as you decide to keep it.

I remember one Christmas Eve my wife and I got into a squabble with some relatives over where we were going to have Christmas dinner. I got into a shouting match on the phone with one of them and things went from bad to worse. The upshot was that nobody came to our house for Christmas Eve, and pretty soon, none of us were talking to each other.

Every time I thought of them after that, or anytime I thought I might run into them, I'd get upset. My heart would pound furiously, and I knew my blood pressure was going through the roof because I didn't want another shouting match.

After about a month of that, I called and apologized for my behavior. I called to end the argument and the grudge. From then on, I was able to think about them without getting upset. I learned that nothing in life is worth jeopardizing my health over and ruining the quality of my life. Even if someone did me wrong, I was not willing to carry a grudge over it.

Carrying a grudge also affects other people. I knew a family in which the father and a son had an ongoing feud. When the family got together, the two wouldn't go near each other. The father wouldn't even go to his grandson's christening. Who paid for that? The mother/

wife had to pay for it, because she loved her husband and son both. The daughters had to pay for it, because they loved both their brother and their father.

Physically, grudges can make you sick. Mentally, every time you think of the other person, you drag up negative feelings and emotions. It's like carrying a bucket of old, dirty oil around with you everywhere you go; it's a mess. You give up your power to the event or the person with whom you are upset. Would you rather be right or happy?

Letting go of grudges is guaranteed to lighten your life. Take the story of Jean, a woman who waited with her husband, Bob, as he was dying. Their daughter Sheri was there, and Sheri's son John, who had come to say goodbye to his grandfather. John hadn't been speaking to his mother; in fact, he had disowned her. Now Jean had all of the emotions of losing her husband along with the concern that John wouldn't talk to his mother Sheri. As it turned out, John hugged his mother, they talked, and he gave her his address and telephone number. Letting go of grudges can begin a whole path of healing.

I know that you can give me a long list of reasons why you should hold onto a grudge. I'm not suggesting that by letting go of a grudge or by forgiving you are condoning the offending behavior. You're just letting go of the emotional attachment to the event.

The mindset in holding a grudge is that you are a victim of the transaction. I invite you to view any given event from the point of view that you created the situation and brought it on yourself to learn a lesson. If you're flexible enough to accept this perception, it will be much easier to let go of your grudge. The only reason you have to hold onto a grudge is to feed your feeling of victimization. By holding onto it, you give power to an event from the past that only exists as a perception in your mind. You can reclaim your power by releasing

A Rose Garden

your need to carry the grudge.

The best example I've ever seen of releasing a grudge was a woman I knew from church, whose son had been run over and killed by several men. During their manslaughter trial, she stood up in the courtroom and forgave them! It's my belief that if she can do that, we can let go of any grudge that we want to!

Exercise:

Who are you holding a grudge against? Call her and tell her you're sorry. Apologize for your role in the dispute without any expectation of how the other person is going to receive it. You are not doing it for her; you are doing it for yourself. If you find it impossible to make that call, or if that person has passed away, let go of the grudge in your heart. Apologize in your mind. Let go of all the pain. As you release the pain, put it in a big pink bubble and watch it float away into space, never again to be seen or heard from again. Celebrate. You have been released from a prison.

Affirmation:

Holding onto a grudge is impossible for me, because I see God in everyone.

Happiness Is a State of Mind

"It's not how much we have, but how much we enjoy that makes happiness." Charles Spurgeon

We are taught to believe that things (a new car, a new home, winning the lottery, etc.) will make us happy. These things and many more can, indeed, make us happy for a while, but that happiness can fade away in minutes. Thus, we find ourselves in a never-ending quest for material things to make us happy.

When we subscribe to the belief that material things make us happy, we are giving up our power to them. When we get them, we are happy, but when we don't, we are unhappy, and once again, we are looking for the next new thing to buy or accomplish to make us happy. It is like being addicted to a drug. We are constantly looking for our next fix.

True happiness comes from within us. It is a state of being, a state of mind. It doesn't require anything from the outside world. We are happy because we exist. We are happy because of who we are, not what we do. Therefore, we are independent of outside influence for our happiness.

How do we learn to subscribe to the point of view that happiness comes from within? First, reject the premise that external things and events make you happy. Second, change your definition of happiness. For example, my definition is that I am happy when I am alive. It doesn't take much to make me happy, now, does it?

The happiness I am talking about is a spiritual happiness. We are happy because we are physical extensions of our creator. This requires an ability to receive His love and feel it and live it. When we can feel

A Rose Garden

the love of God and accept that we are worthy of it, we can go about everything in our lives as though that is all that matters. The beauty of this is that we don't have to do anything to earn it. It is a gift from God that lasts forever. All we have to do is to accept it. This requires that we focus on it. It is kind of like sun bathing. When we lie in the sun, we close our eyes and just feel the warmth of the sun. Similarly, in a state of happiness, we can close our eyes and feel the warmth of God surrounding us, no matter what is going on in our physical lives.

The choice is to either constantly pursue temporary happiness by going after physical things that make us happy or go deeper and open our hearts, minds and spirits to the love God has for us. That's when we will feel and experience true happiness.

Exercise:

Think of the event that has made you the happiest in your entire life. Get in touch with your feelings about it; see it, touch it, hear it, smell it and taste it. What was the temperature? What did the air feel like? Imagine that the whole world has gathered to honor you and your life and all you have accomplished. Increase the intensity of this thought as much as you possibly can. Go inside and open your heart to God's happiness and know that it is greater than anything you can imagine. Feel it and know that this is your gift forever. You can stay here permanently or you can come back here whenever you want to. You now have created your eternal state of bliss. Enjoy it; it is your birthright.

Affirmation:

I choose to express and experience my divine birthright of an inner happiness from God.

Part 4

Points of View to Help You Successfully Navigate Through Life

A Rose Garden

You Will Learn Lessons*

"Life is a language in which certain truths are conveyed to us; if we could learn them in some other way we should not live."
Arthur Schopenhauer

How many people do you know who have been twice divorced? Why did this happen? Because they didn't learn the lessons that their first spouses were put into their lives to teach them! Let me put it in another way: Everyone we meet in life is there for two reasons: to teach us something and to learn something from us. We don't have to be concerned with what we are there to teach them, but we do have to be concerned about what they are here to teach us.

What are others trying to teach you? Maybe it's patience, compassion, tolerance or self-acceptance. In order to answer this, you must be as objective as possible. If we don't learn lessons from others, it is guaranteed that you will attract someone else into your life who will try to teach them to you. The fact is you will learn the lesson, or it will keep presenting itself to you!

You don't have to believe me; just take a look at your life. If something happened to you only once, ask yourself what that event taught you, because you evidently learned that lesson the first time, and you were able to move on to the next lesson. If different people keep coming into your life with the same problem, stop reacting to them in disgust or anger. Remove yourself from them emotionally and ask what they are there to teach you.

If you don't accept that one of life's purposes is to learn lessons, then you see yourself as a victim of your life experiences. Consequently, you will never understand the principle of cause and effect. The cause is your thoughts and beliefs. The effect is the event that you consider a tragedy. By learning the lesson, you change your thoughts and beliefs, which changes future events.

Accept the fact that you are no less of a person because you make mistakes. Mistakes are the way you learn and grow, and that's why you're here. You can learn your lessons the easy way or the hard way, but you cannot choose not to learn them!

Exercise:

Identify the area of your life where you have had the most difficulty and made the least progress. Think of one event that particularly frustrated you. I am now going to hire you to consult with yourself to identify the lessons there are in this event. I am trying to get you to remove yourself emotionally and look at it objectively. Look at it as if it happened to someone else and you had the inside knowledge to render an expert opinion. What are the lessons of this event or relationship? How can you implement them in your life? Commit to finding the lesson in all of your relationships. Know that you attract people into your life to teach you lessons.

Affirmation:

I am a magnet that attracts great people to teach me life lessons! I am grateful to these teachers. They are here to help me find my way back to my creator.

(Footnotes)
* Fom the Poem <u>The Rules for Being Human</u> by anonymous

A Rose Garden

A Lesson Is Repeated Until it Is Learned*

"Live to learn and you will learn to live." Portuguese proverb

Hopefully, our life experiences have taught us already that lessons will be repeated until they are learned. I learned this fact while working in my teens and twenties. Someone at work would irritate me, but when I moved on to another job, someone there would irritate me as well. Finally, I realized that the ways some people view life are contrary to my views. When I learned to accept others' views of life as being valid, the lesson was learned.

Who irritates you the most? Your challenge is to see him as your greatest teacher! By allowing him to irritate you, upset you, make you angry, hurt your feelings, etc., you give your power to him. He is just being himself, because that's all he knows how to be. When you can accept him as he is and accept yourself as you are, you become an observer of life.

When you learn what you need to learn from that person, you will go on to the next person or the next event to learn the next lesson. When you don't learn it, the lesson repeats itself. The person may look different and the events may change, but the lesson is still there. It's like going to a masquerade party; there are always people underneath the costumes. The trick is to constantly remind yourself that others are here to teach you something. Once you accept this premise, the lessons become easier. But as long as you are resistant to it, you won't learn lessons, and they will keep presenting themselves. Learning lessons can be easy or hard. The choice is yours.

Exercise:

Which lesson have you had the hardest time learning? Once you've identified it, sit quietly and think about how you need to look at that lesson in order to learn. What elements would you need to incorporate into your personality or belief system in order to learn it? Spend some time on this lesson, because once you learn it, your entire life will shift. You'll understand why you're here, which will make it easier to change your perceptions, attitudes and behaviors.

Affirmation:

I use my skills to easily learn my life lessons.

(Footnotes)
* Fom the Poem <u>The Rules for Being Human</u> by anonymous.

A Rose Garden

There Are No Mistakes—Only Lessons*

"There are no mistakes, no coincidences. All events are blessings given to us to learn." Elizabeth Kubler-Ross

Growth is a process of trial and error. The failed experiments are as much a part of the process as the experiment that ultimately works. For example, every time we get into a car, we constantly adjust the steering wheel as we drive. We don't think of those adjustments as mistakes, but they are necessary to keep the car going in the direction that we want it to go. Life is exactly the same; it is a constant series of adjustments. Circumstances are changing every day, and it's important for us to adjust to them without too much drama.

When my friend Gina gets cut off by another driver on the freeway, her attitude is, "I don't want to get into that energy." How would your life change if there was no drama, no ego, no pride or no fear? This would require a willingness to let go, a willingness to not have to be right. It requires a mindset of being. By experimenting, we get to see where our limits are and how we make those adjustments. Without drama, you can view every event in your life as an experiment.

Many people are afraid to make mistakes, because they get criticized for them or are seen as failures. Changing your definition of failure can help. Just decide that every time you try, you are a success. You can also eliminate your fear of being criticized by adopting the title philosophy of Terry Cole Whitaker's book *What You Think of Me is None of My Business*. When we are concerned about other people's criticisms, then we criticize ourselves. There is a tremendous sense of freedom when you accept yourself just as you are.

Exercise:

Identify an area in your life where you feel stuck. What would you have to believe about this area in order for it to flow smoothly, without any impediments? Identify at least three actions that you can take to implement this belief in your life. For one day, try doing everything without attaching any drama to it.

Affirmation:

I am grateful for the lessons that are presented to me. I embrace these lessons as gifts of wisdom, knowledge and experience that make me richer, fuller, more complete and more of a divine being.

(Footnotes)
* Fom the Poem <u>The Rules for Being Human</u> by anonymous.

A Rose Garden

Life's Greatest Periods of Growth Usually Follow Life's Tragedies

"The key to growth is the introduction of higher levels of consciousness into our awareness."
Pir Vilayat Inayat Khan

If you looked back on the hardest times of your life, you would probably notice that those times were followed by some of the greatest personal growth periods of your life. There's never a right time for tragedies to occur, but we have to trust in the process of life and know that those are times for us to grow.

When tragedies occur, we want to get away from the pain as fast as we can. One of the lessons that we're called to learn is to simply be with the pain and feel it. The only way out of the pain is to go through it. We live in a world of duality, and in order to experience ecstasy, we must experience pain. Know that the ecstasy is just on the other side of the pain.

Although the following story is not a story of tragedy, it perfectly illustrates the way that fear and resistance can hold you back from experiencing the gifts in a situation. I once took a class that met, one weekend a month for nine months, in Salt Lake City. However, in February, we met in Idaho. They told us to bring our bathing suit, because there was a great spa outside. Well, I resisted that because I couldn't imagine walking outside in the snow in a bathing suit, getting wet and then walking back to the lodge in the cold and the snow. I decided to take a bathing suit anyway.

Each group had to do an exercise. One group decided they were going to do an exercise around the pool. I put on my swimsuit, pants, thermal socks, shoes jacket and my gloves and walked up to the pool.

As part of the exercise, we were figuratively throwing all of our dreams into the pool. When we completed that it was time to take off our clothes and go into the pool—into our dreams. The fact that this pool was heated to 106° didn't lessen my anxiety one bit when I started to take off my clothes to go into the pool. The last thing I took off was my socks.

The 15 to 20 seconds I stood on that cold cement in the snow, barefooted I experienced the most excruciating physical pain of my life. It was like I was standing on a bed of nails. I walked to the ladder and walked into the pool, and began to experience the most remarkable transformation in my life. The 106-degree water brought a complete sense of calm and peace. The snowflakes dancing on to my forehead and fluttering into my eyelashes was like being in a dream. Had I allowed my fear of being cold to stop me from going through with that experiment, I never would have reached the ecstasy of being in a pool in the snow for the first time in my life.

Do not allow your fear to paralyze you or to create a barrier that we'll preclude you from experiencing the ecstasy. Know that you will live through it and gain a deeper sense of wisdom from it. Be careful not to allow your disappointment or anger to turn to bitterness, which effectively locks the door and stops your opportunity to grow.

Tragedy is a call to learn, which can happen in different time frames. But for now, focus on learning from the events of the past. You have the ability to go back into any event with all of your emotions and learn what it had to offer.

Exercise:

Think of a tragic event from your life and view it in your mind as if you were watching it from a seat in a movie theatre. If the emotions

A Rose Garden

from the event are too strong to relive, watch the tragedy from the balcony of the theater. If this is still too intense, visualize yourself in an airplane, looking down on yourself in the balcony as you watch the tragedy. Identify what you learned from that tragedy and how you have changed.

Affirmation:

Life is my teacher, and my most profound lessons come disguised as tragedies.

Others Are Mirrors of You*

"O you who are seeking God, know this: Know that we are the mirror of God, the absolute truth." Nu' Ali Shah

You cannot love or hate something about another person unless it reflects something you love or hate about yourself. You may be quick to judge others, finding things you don't like about them. But you can be absolutely sure that they are also things you don't like about yourself! Otherwise, you wouldn't see them. The reason we see them in others is that it is easier to see things that are reflected to us than it is to see them in ourselves. We aren't objective about ourselves. We only see what we want to see. And we don't go around looking for the lessons we need to learn. Life shows us what we haven't learned yet by allowing us to glimpse problems in other people's lives.

When you see an undesirable trait in another person, the first thing to do is ask yourself if you possess that same quality. Let's say the other person is selfish. You might be tempted to say, "I'm not really selfish or self-centered." But a better question is, "How am *I* self-centered?" Then ask, "What can I do to become less self-centered?"

Don't beat up on yourself because you see yourself with such character traits. They are simply life's way of showing you what lessons you have to learn. You give your power away by saying that they're not problems for you.

When you see a flaw in someone, mentally thank her for bringing this lesson to your attention. Be sure that you don't attach any emotion to your observation. Simply say, "Here is an area of my life on which I need to focus my attention. There is something here for me to learn." Remember that all of us are students of life and our sole purpose is to

A Rose Garden

learn the lessons that life presents us. It is not our job to judge them but to simply observe them.

Accepting that others are merely mirrors of you is a tremendous gift. It enables you to see what lessons you have to learn and which ones you have already learned. To maximize the learning potential, it is crucial that you release any emotional attachment to what you observe in someone.

Let's say that your boss is taking advantage of you. The first tendency is to get upset about being abused. Instead, ask, "Who am I taking advantage of in my life? How am I taking advantage of them? What action do I need to take to stop? Very gently and unemotionally go to work learning this lesson. If no one ever takes advantage of you again, then you have learned the lesson. If it happens again, then ask the questions again. Don't beat up on yourself for not having learned the lesson. Life is a process, not an event. Be gentle and loving with yourself. You will make mistakes your entire life. That is part of being human. The key is what you learn from these mistakes.

Exercise:

With whom do you have the hardest time getting along? First ask yourself what about her upsets you the most. Where is this trait manifesting itself in your life? Note: "It isn't" is not an acceptable answer. If you are having trouble seeing this trait in yourself, go to your best friend and ask him to show you. What action can you take to stop acting that way? Keep track of your progress and reward yourself when you succeed. Be gentle with yourself. Remember that you are a student of life, not a master of life. When you become a master, you will no longer need a body.

Affirmation:

I love the opportunity for other people show me what I haven't perfected in my life yet.

(Footnotes)
* Fom the Poem <u>The Rules for Being Human</u> by anonymous.

A Rose Garden
What You Make of Your Life Is up to You*

"Life is what we make it, and the world is what we make it. The eyes of the cheerful and of the melancholy man are fixed upon the same creation: but very different are the aspects, which it bears to them."
Albert Pike

We have all the tools and resources we need to do what we want with our lives. What we do with these tools and resources is up to us. No one dictates to us. We are not victims of circumstances. It's our attitudes, beliefs and our ability to reprogram our subconscious minds that enable us to create what we want in life.

Some of you have lists of reasons why you won't make more of your talent: "I'm too old to change," "I don't have enough education," "I'm tired," "Life has beaten me up." We feel sorry for ourselves and have our little pity parties, to which we invite all our friends. They go along with us and feel sorry for us. A true friend, however, would kick us in the bottom and say, "Get on with it! I'm really tired of you cheating me out of the opportunity to know and experience the incredible gift that you are."

Don't waste time lamenting why you aren't further along or more successful in your life. Susan Shepard once told me that "Why?" is the booby prize. It doesn't matter why you aren't more successful. Accept that you aren't and that the reason is because you aren't ready. Also accept the fact that you are ready to make more of your life than you ever have before. In that readiness, you acknowledge that the past has nothing to do with the present and absolutely nothing at all to do with the creation of your future. What you do with your life is up to you. It's your choice.

Exercise:

Identify the area of your life you want to change the most. Write down all the things you want in this area. Write in great detail, write rapidly, write without thinking, and write without lifting your pen. Don't think; just keep writing for five minutes. What resources will you need to get those things? List all the resources you have. Don't be shy here; be bold, brave, courageous, and confident. Dig down deep inside yourself to know who you are. This is an Easter egg hunt. It will be one of the most important discoveries you make in your life. After you have written all of these resources down, prioritize them. Identify the three most important resources that you will need in order to create your future in this area. Develop an action plan for how you're going to use those three resources every day to realize your goal. Cut pictures out of magazines and develop a collage that illustrates what you want this area of your life to look like. I promise that you if you do this, you will get what you want.

Affirmation:

I use all of my gifts and talents to be all that I can be.

(Footnotes)
* Fom the Poem <u>The Rules for Being Human</u> by anonymous.

A Rose Garden

Keep It Simple

"The greatest results in life are usually attained by simple means and the exercise of ordinary qualities. These for the most part may be summed up in these two: commonsense and perseverance."
Owen Feltham

In order for many of us to have a higher sense of self esteem we complicate simple things. In our minds that makes us more intelligent, more important, indispensable, intelligent, sophisticated, or knowledgeable. I believe that the most important things in life are very simple.

An overwhelming majority of our time is spent communicating. One of our responsibilities in our communication is to communicate so that it's impossible for you to be misunderstood. Simplify your message. Our goal in our communication is not to drain people. Our goal should be to find a way to fill them up, show them a way to see the value in themselves no matter what we're interacting about. If I'm teaching you something, I want to show you how easy it for you not only to comprehend it, and to incorporate it into your life. There's nothing difficult about it. The ego's responsibility is to always ensure that life is complicated that it's a state of chaos. Whenever we're unsettled, we know ego is in charge.

Life can be simple. Allow it to be simple, keep it simple. Know that the purpose of your life is to learn lessons. Focus on the lesson the experience is trying to teach you.

Robert Fulghum, author of *All I Really Need to Know I Learned in Kindergarten*, has most elegantly simplified his own lessons in life to the basics, my favorites of which I've listed here:

Share everything.

Play fair.

Don't hit people.

Put things back where you found them.

Clean up your own mess.

Don't take things that aren't yours.

Say you're sorry when you hurt somebody.

Wash your hands before you eat.

Flush.

I encourage you to buy Fulghum's book—it's a classic.

Exercise:

Think about the last time you had a communication problem with someone—whether it was with a family member, someone at the checkout stand, or a business associate. Write down a couple things that you said in that communication that you think were misunderstood. Now, see how you can simplify what you said without losing the meaning and without sounding harsh. For one day after you say something to somebody ask them what they heard you say. Then adjust your communication based on their feedback.

Affirmation:

My messages to others are simple and kind.

A Rose Garden

See Life Through Rose-Colored Glasses

"Beauty is in the eye of the beholder." Margaret Wolfe Hungerford

Author Michael Gerber has said that everyone has a point of view and that we spend all our waking moments looking for evidence to support that point of view. If you believe everyone is out to get you, then when someone actually does, you'll probably say, "See? I told you everyone is out to get me." There may have been 10,000 events in your life since the last time someone "got you," but you have chosen only to focus on that one time that someone wronged you.

In *Blessings from the Other Side*, Silvia Browne says that "when we plan our lives, we are given a choice of seven option lines to choose from: love, health, finance, career, spirituality, family and social life. The option line we decide on is the area of this earthly school that we've decided to major in, the area we'll agonize over the most, and the area we feel we have the most to learn."

In other words, the area you have chosen for growth and learning is directly dependent upon how you choose to study it. Will you make it easy and fun, or will it be a struggle? If you choose to make it a struggle, why do that? Is it because you believe life is hard and a struggle? If so, you can always choose now to make it easy. You can wake up tomorrow and believe that life is wonderful and that everyone is here to help you live the perfect life. It is your choice.

For example, when we are in love, we see only the good and beauty in the other person. But that romantic love ends, and things that used to be cute become aggravating. The other person's behavior didn't change; only the way we interpreted it changed.

To enjoy life to the fullest, we have to look at the actions of the people in our lives with lightness and love, tolerance and acceptance. Who we are and how we behave is part of our charm. Look for the charm in every person you meet. Become an observer of actions, not the judge. When we judge others, we are only judging ourselves. Accept yourself just the way you are, and accept everyone else in your life just the way they are.

Exercise:

Buy a pair of rose-colored glasses. Look for the beauty in every person you encounter! You will find what you are looking for and only what you look for. When you encounter unpleasant behavior, believe that the other person is asking you for love.

Affirmation:

There is beauty in every person, every event, and I see it everywhere I go!

A Rose Garden

Life Is Never What It Seems to Be

"It was the best of times; it was the worst of times." Charles Dickens

Most of us evaluate the status of our lives based on what we see externally. If we have good jobs and our careers are progressing and everything is going smoothly with our families, then we say that life is great. On the other hand, if we are out of work, having cash-flow problems, in a rocky marriage or are feeling sick, then we think life is really rough. Sometimes we even get angry with God and say, "Why me?"

Think of God as your master teacher and trust Him implicitly. When something bad happens, go inside and know that God sent this to you to teach you a lesson. Likewise, when things are going smoothly, be grateful and know that you are being given the opportunity to take a break from life lessons. But always be ready. You never know when the next lesson will start.

At times when I've asked God, "Why am I sitting here with major cash-flow problems and no visible means of support coming in?" His answer was, "This is where I want you to be." I thought about that and wondered why He wanted me to be here. The answer that came to me was that this was exactly where I needed to be in order for the messages of this book to come through me. It also occurred to me that I was too attached to the outcomes of my actions. Incredible insights have come through me that can be applied to my life and my journey. My purpose is to do the work and then allow the outcomes to unfold however they will.

Life is not about what is happening in your external world. It is about what is happening to you internally. How are you growing spiritually? Are you learning new ways to love unconditionally? Are you open to absorbing life's wisdom? Are you conscious of the path you are on? How can you go deeper into yourself and discover your essence? What is your purpose?

The external events in our lives are the means by which we learn the internal lessons that we came into this world to learn. The external events have nothing to do with material possessions, success, sickness or death. They only occur because we have chosen to occupy bodies that are governed by the five senses. Therefore, our lessons are manifested in the realm of the five senses so that we might be able to grasp them.

Life is not what it appears to be on the outside. And it doesn't matter whether the outside looks good or bad. Don't judge based on appearances. Just accept and release your attachment to the outcomes.

Exercise:

Think of a painful experience in your life and write about it in detail. How did you interpret the event at the time? What did you learn from that event? How have you grown from the event? What meaning do you give to this event today? If you are too close to the event emotionally, wait awhile and try again later.

Affirmation:

I am an eager student of life. I am excited about learning my lessons. I completely trust my teacher.

A Rose Garden

Accept Yourself and Others Just As You Are

"This above all; to thine own self be true." William Shakespeare

Do you want people to change you, or would you rather be accepted just the way you are? The way to get others to accept you the way you are is to accept them the way they are. This is unconditional love.

Let's start by talking about accepting ourselves. Many people don't accept themselves because of their physical features, education, sense of humor, status in life, job, etc. But behind everything we reject about ourselves is a belief. Think of a specific trait and ask yourself what your beliefs are about people who exhibit that trait. Now ask yourself what your beliefs need to be in order to accept that trait within yourself. It may help to stand in front of a mirror stark naked and say to yourself, "I love you. You're beautiful." You may be tempted to reject yourself because you think some features are unacceptable. Continue saying "I love you. You are beautiful" until you see into your soul and the beauty shining from within. Then you can marvel at your beauty, because you have discovered the source.

The next challenge is to accept others the way they are. Before we can do that, we have to stop judging others and ourselves. Become one who observes life. If you can see something as just existing rather than possessing a positive or negative charge, it is very simple to accept it the way it is. The personalities we have will best enable us to learn the lessons we came to learn. When we do, our personalities change. Just observe others' personalities and accept that they are the ones that are best suited for helping those people learn lessons.

Your challenge is to accept others' points of view as valid for them.

You don't have to embrace them as your points of view, but you need to try to see life the way others see theirs, because they value themselves and their points of view.

We all came into the world able to love unconditionally. When we were babies, it didn't matter what people looked like; we loved them all the same. This was a gift we were given when we came into this world. You can reclaim your birthright any time you desire. Simply accept yourself as a divine child of God with all the rights and privileges that are part of your divine inheritance.

Exercise:

Who do you have the hardest time accepting? What do you have to believe about that person to accept them just the way they are?

Affirmation:

I love and accept myself just the way I am, and I love and accept everyone else just the way they are.

A Rose Garden

Don't Judge

"The observation of others is coloured by our inability to observe ourselves impartially. We can never be impartial about anything until we can be impartial about our own organism." A.R. Orage

We tend to pass judgment on ourselves and others, but one of the big challenges of life is to be an observer. Try to just observe a twenty-year-old car with a lot of dents and rust. Simply observe a purple house. Observe a person who is five feet, two inches tall and weighs 300 pounds. Learn to observe without judging whether something is good or bad.

When we make judgments about things, we compare those things to ourselves and then judge ourselves as either better or worse. This creates a win-lose situation. But every win-lose situation is a lose-lose situation. Our goal is to only create win-win situations. The truth is that nothing is better than anything else. Everything is the same. There isn't a single human being God ever created or ever will create whom He loves more than you, whether it's the Pope, the Dalai Lama, the president of the United States, the queen of England, Osama bin Laden or a homeless person.

Judging does not serve us. It never can, it never did, and it never will. There's no value in judging other than to separate yourself. When we separate ourselves from the rest of humanity, we weaken ourselves, isolate ourselves and lose contact with our creator and with the divine aspect of ourselves. Consider making a private vow that you will try never to judge again.

Release yourself from the burden of judging everything and I guarantee that you will be a more joyful person. You'll enjoy your life immeasurably more because you chose not to give any meaning to things that you observed. You will also have more power, because judging causes emotions that have a negative impact on your quality of life

Exercise:

Promise yourself that you will stop judging. Notice when you do find yourself being judgmental and renew your commitment to stopping.

Affirmation:

I love observing life.

A Rose Garden

The Answers Lie Within You*

"He who reigns within himself and rules passions, desires, and fears is more than a king." John Milton

I'm always looking to somebody else for my answers. I've got a coach, a psychic friend, a psychologist friend, and I'm constantly asking, "What do I do?" The reason this happens is that I don't trust my intuition. In order for me to overcome these obstacles, I meditate and try to get in touch with my intuition.

This reminds me of the story about the woman crawling around on her hands and knees underneath a street light. A man comes up to her and asks, "What are you looking for?" She says, "I'm looking for my house key." He asks, "Did you drop it out here?" She says, "No, I dropped it in the house, but the light is better out here!"

This, of course, is an absurd example, but when we look at our own lives, we see that we look for answers in all the wrong places. We look for other people, other circumstances and other times, and we don't see the absurdity of it. It seems perfectly logical to us, because we're scared and insecure, and we allow our egos to keep our lives in a state of chaos. But if our focus is on continuously staying in connection with our highest selves, then we can believe and trust that what we're looking for lies within us.

Exercise:

Think of an unresolved issue in your life. Mediate and ask yourself, "How do I handle this situation?" The answer will come to you. It may not be today or tomorrow or next week or next month, but be patient and persistent and have absolute faith that you will receive the answer. This will require being quiet and listening. Listen with your ears, eyes and heart. When you hear the answer, trust it. Don't judge it. Don't interpret it. Simply accept it.

Affirmation:

I turn within to my divine connection to receive the answers to all my questions.

(Footnotes)
* Fom the Poem <u>The Rules for Being Human</u> by anonymous.

A Rose Garden

Your Power Lies Within You

"It matters not how straight the gate, how charged with punishment the scroll, I am the master of my fate: I am the captain of my soul."
William Henley

It seems that we are always finding new ways to give away our power, whether it's by allowing someone else's opinion of us to affect our opinion of ourselves or by getting upset by criticism. We give away our power by seeing ourselves as victims, by judging other people, blaming others, allowing people to intimidate us, not believing in ourselves, living in fear, not believing in the miraculous power of God, holding grudges, not forgiving others, and the list goes on and on.

Know that you have all the power, wisdom, knowledge, insight, and skills you need to learn who you really are. Don't be afraid to go inside and discover yourself. Find your power, trust it, and allow it to come out and express itself fully, knowing that it will be for your highest good and for the good of everyone whose lives you touch.

Stop looking toward other people to validate your sense of self-worth. Look within yourself, forgive yourself for everything you've ever done, get in touch with your power, and be sensitive to your intuition and your ability to create.

Exercise:

Make a list of the ways you give your power away. Choose an area of your life in which you would like to reclaim your power. As an example, let's say that you tend to blame others for the things that happen in your life. Promise yourself that you will stop blaming others. Accept the responsibility for creating the situations you have brought into your life. When you are tempted to blame somebody, simply say,

"I created this to teach myself something. What is it?" Accept that you brought that person into your life to choreograph an event that will teach you the lesson you need to learn. When you learn the lesson, either the person will change or he/she will disappear.

Affirmation:

God is the source of my power. He lies within me, and I know that all of my power lies within me, that all wisdom and all answers are within me. I willingly retreat within myself for the answers to all the questions in my life.

A Rose Garden

Part 5

Beliefs That Will Enable You to Experience Life Fully

A Rose Garden

Love Yourself

"Love is an image of God and not a lifeless image, but the living essence of the divine nature, which beams full of all goodness."
Martin Luther

When we truly love ourselves, all of life's other lessons come so much easier. If we operate from that premise that we are divine beings in physical bodies and that we have come here to learn lessons, then we are going to be much more successful, because we will recognize when the ego is in control, and we will banish it.

The function of the higher self is to seek peace, but the ego's job is to keep life in a constant state of chaos. Ego is always trying to make sure that we get credit for accomplishments. It always wants us to be right, hold grudges, get angry and get even. In other words, if you aren't at peace, then your ego is in charge.

When we love ourselves, it is much easier to recognize when the ego is in charge. We thank it for its efforts and dismiss it. Then we ask the question, "How would God respond to this situation?" The answer is always, "with love." When we are in a state of peace, it is infinitely simpler to look for and find the lessons that need to be learned.

How do you love yourself? Let's start with how *not* to love yourself. For example, you are not just your body type or your job title or the amount of money you have. You don't love yourself when you are angry, hostile, resentful, vengeful, prejudiced or judgmental. You don't love yourself when you withhold love from others, when you abuse yourself or others, when you are fearful, when you believe in scarcity or when you don't forgive yourself or someone else.

If you see yourself in any of these behaviors and are starting to think that you must not love yourself very much, remember that life is a process. You are in the process of learning to love yourself, no matter what.

Now, let's shift our focus from what we shouldn't be to what we should be.

We are divine physical extensions of God, having a physical experience in our own individual lives. In a sense, we are God! If you take a bucket of water out of the ocean, is it still the ocean? Of course it is. It has all of the properties of the ocean except that it doesn't have the same volume. Therefore, it can do all the things that the ocean can do, only in smaller quantities. God loves us unconditionally! There is nothing that we can do or say that will change His love for us. Our challenge now is to love ourselves, no matter what we say or do.

Love yourself, no matter your size, weight, color, age, sex, education, financial status or job title. Love yourself whether you are the president of the United States or a homeless person. Love yourself whether you are a billionaire or penniless. You are only here for a visit! Your value as a divine being in a human body has nothing to do with anything physical.

Easier said than done, you may be thinking. In fact, it can be very easy. You have an image of who you are, and if you measure up to it, then you can love yourself; if not, then you can't. My suggestion is that you change your self-image and the definition of when you can love yourself. You are a divine being whose worth cannot be measured by worldly possessions or traits! You are not a physical body trying out for a part in life. You are already God, and God is love! God doesn't do love; He is love. That is why we are called human *beings*. We cannot *do* anything to earn God's love—we only have to *be* who we already are. God loves us unconditionally. That means there is nothing we can say

A Rose Garden

or do to change His love for us. So our challenge is to love ourselves, no matter what we say or do.

When we were babies, we were loved unconditionally. Then our parents developed expectations of us. When we met them, we received their love and approval. When we didn't meet their expectations, we didn't get their love and approval. As adults, we have learned to love ourselves the same way. If we do good things and are successful, then we love ourselves. If we make mistakes or fail, then we don't love ourselves. What is worse is that we beat up on or hate ourselves. Then we treat other people just as poorly.

The key is to change your image of yourself and love yourself, no matter what you say or do!

Exercise:

Make a list of what makes you lovable. Define all of the requirements you have placed on yourself in order for you to love yourself. In your mind, discard all of these requirements. Replace them with this new definition of what makes you lovable: I am lovable because I am.

Affirmation:

I always love myself! I am love.

Forgive Yourself and Others

"Love thy neighbor as thy self. Do not to others what thou wouldst not wish to be done to thyself. Forgive injuries. Forgive thy enemy, be reconciled to him, give him assistance, and invoke God in his behalf."
Confucius

What price do you pay for holding on to the anger, guilt, pain or suffering that you carry around? The price can vary from physical or mental pain to disease, severed relationships or even death! Do not underestimate the cost of not forgiving someone or yourself. You may be thinking, "But you don't know what that person did to me!" No, I don't, and I am not trying to minimize the impact of whatever is causing such pain. But not forgiving will not change the event. It has happened, and it can never be undone. Furthermore, forgiveness does not require that you condone the behavior!

Why should you forgive? For yourself! You forgive for your peace of mind and health, not for the other person. You can come up with all kinds of excuses for why you shouldn't forgive someone. This doesn't mean that you have to pick up the phone and forgive a murderer or rapist. But you can forgive him in your heart! That is where you are carrying the pain. When you refuse to forgive others, you are acting as the judge, the jury and the executioner.

A friend of mine had a twenty-four-year-old son who died while being robbed. In the courtroom, my friend stood up and forgave the culprits! My goal is to help you find it in your heart to forgive the actions that are causing so much pain in your life and begin the process of healing. Honor yourself by having the grace to let go! What is done is done. Get on with your life and discover what you can learn from the event. For many of us, the hardest people in the world to forgive are ourselves!

A Rose Garden

Why is that so hard? Do you believe you have to be perfect? Do you think that you are so unworthy that you don't deserve to be forgiven? How arrogant. You are a physical extension of God. Therefore, everything is forgivable. My belief is that God doesn't need to forgive us for anything, because in God's view, there is no right or wrong. Everything just is.

Forgiving yourself means letting go of your past. You are not your past. You are not your behavior. Your behavior is there to teach you. It is part of the journey back to your creator. Nothing is right or wrong! There are just events in your life to help you find your way home! Learn from them, release them, forgive yourself, and move on with your life. Learn to embrace your mistakes and see them as great teachers. Thank them for the lessons they have taught you.

There is no one God has ever created whom He loves more than you. We have no idea how much God loves us. This unconditional love is a supreme gift. There is nothing we have to do to earn it, and there is nothing we can do to lose it. Find this love, feel this love, and out of honor for it, forgive yourself so you can go about the work you came here to do. You are on a mission, and you cannot do you best work until you forgive yourself for the mistakes you made in trying to find your way home to your creator.

Once I was told, "Let go of the past." I asked how. The answer was, "Take a pen, make a fist around it, and hold your arm straight out. Stand there until the pain of holding on exceeds the pain of letting go. Then you can let go." Forgiveness is giving up all hope for a better past.

If a baby spits up on you, you don't get angry with her or hold a grudge against her or punish her. She didn't do anything wrong. She was just being a baby. We are just the same. We are just human beings. When we can't forgive someone or ourselves, we are being judgmental.

It is not your job to be a judge. Nothing positive can come out of it. Give yourself the greatest gift you can: Forgive yourself and everyone who has ever done wrong by you. Release them, let them go, and send them love as they leave. After all, they, too, are God.

Exercise:

Make a list of everyone you have not forgiven as well as the reasons why you haven't. Go someplace where you won't be interrupted and see each person in your mind's eye. Say, "_____, I forgive you for _____. I release you and let you go in love." Do this for fifteen minutes at a time. Repeat this process often, two or three times a year for the rest of your life.

Affirmation:

I give up all hope for a better past. I forgive everyone (including myself) who has hurt me.

A Rose Garden

Believe in Yourself

"Nurture your minds with great thoughts. To believe in the heroic make heroes." Disraeli

Most of us have never been taught to believe in ourselves. We have been taught to be humble. When someone compliments us, we minimize it more often than not. If someone tells us we are great, we believe that our accepting the compliment makes us braggarts. The truth is that we don't believe in ourselves.

In contrast, look at Muhammad Ali. He believed in himself. He told himself over and over again how much he believed in himself, and then he showed the entire world how great he was!

The first reason you don't believe in yourself is that nobody has ever given you permission to do so. So I will. I give you permission to believe in yourself. Believe in yourself, no matter what evidence there is to the contrary.

There is nobody that God has ever created whom He loves more than you, and He has never given anyone the gifts He has given you. What is asked of you is to use these gifts. In order to do that, you have to believe they exist, and you must believe in yourself.

The second reason you don't believe in yourself is that nobody has given you a reason to believe in yourself. Now I am giving you a reason: The world is incomplete without you at your best. In order for you to be your best, you must believe in yourself. We are just waiting for you to stand up and claim your greatness.

Why should you believe in yourself? Because you are a unique creation of God. The world is incomplete without you functioning as the complete you. We need you to believe in yourself so we can reach our fullest selves. There is only one consciousness, and it depends on your being the best you can in order for it to achieve its unlimited destiny.

The third reason you don't believe in yourself is that you are afraid to. Adopt the mindset, "I must believe in myself. The world is counting on me and I will not let it down. I love and respect life and God too much to play life as a midget when I am a giant."

Believe in yourself and the whole world will believe in you. Jesus believed in Himself. His belief was so strong that He was put to death. Yet 2000 years later, people still believe in Him. Buddha, Mohammed, Abraham Lincoln, Martin Luther King, Jr. all believed in themselves and their missions. Their beliefs were so strong that they sacrificed their lives for them. I am not suggesting that if you believe in yourself you will necessarily die for it, but when you believe in yourself, you will begin to live your greatness.

The world will change immensely when enough of us believe in ourselves. For years, I didn't believe that I could write. Now I believe it and am allowing the divine influence to come through me and write something that will make all of us better human beings. Our lives will be better for it, and we will change the consciousness of the human race. All of this will happen because we decided to believe in ourselves. What will happen when you put your belief in yourself into action?

Exercise:

Write down what you believe about yourself now. Then write down what you would have to believe in order for you to believe in yourself.

Affirmation:

I am making a positive difference in the world.

A Rose Garden

Be True to Yourself

"Our own hearts, not other men's opinions, form our true honor."
Samuel Coleridge

We compromise ourselves in so many ways: to make a living, to raise a family, to spare others' feelings, to keep the peace, to avoid conflict. Why do we do all these things? Because we believe that the cost of not doing them exceeds the cost of doing them. In other words, we believe that it would be less expensive to do what we have to do to keep our jobs, to keep peace in the family or to avoid conflict than it would be to be true to ourselves.

What are some of the ways we can be true to ourselves? Let's start with our work environment. Let's say you're asked to do something that violates your ethics, such as lying, cheating or stealing. How might you rationalize doing any of these things? By saying, "I need my job, I'm close to retirement, I need the health benefits." But what is the price you would pay? Your integrity.

Or let's say you have a spouse who physically or mentally abuses you, intimidates you or doesn't allow you to express your opinion. You say, "I allow that, because I have to be here for the children. I don't want to create a scene. It's easier to just give in than it is to stand up for myself." When you say that, you're compromising your integrity, and the cost is enormous. It is a loss of self. You no longer value yourself as a human being; instead you value money, fear, security and peace.

But what you're also doing is losing sight of your life's purpose, which is to learn. Let's look at a situation where an employer asks you to be dishonest or to violate your ethics. What lesson can you learn from this? Sometimes there are conflicting lessons. One may be just to ignore things that people say. The other may be to respect yourself. Tell yourself, "I have to love myself. I must be true to myself. This has nothing to do with my employer. I created this situation to come into my life so that I can decide if I truly respect myself. If I do have a sense of self-worth, I will not accept this."

Of course, that's when fear/ego come in and say, "If you don't do what you're being asked, you're going to get fired." That's when you invite Spirit in and say, "Spirit, guide me to have the wisdom to do what is right in this situation. Give me the strength and the confidence to know that by doing what is right, you will guide me to something higher and better than what I have now. In this I trust, I believe, I surrender." Now let's look at the example in which you are being abused by your husband. You may believe the children are better served by having two parents rather than one. But what if your children created a life plan to be with a single mother? By accepting and staying in the abusive relationship, you are depriving them of the plan they came to execute. You are saying that being raised by a single mom is not a lesson they need to learn. You are teaching them not to demand respect for themselves and that abuse is acceptable. Then there would be a good chance that they would go on to abuse their own children. All these negative thoughts are your ego doing its work. Always remember to invite the Spirit in and ask your higher self what the best thing is for all concerned.

Being true to yourself means loving yourself, respecting yourself, taking care of yourself, knowing when to say no, knowing when to go along, and when not to go along. What if the purpose of your life was to determine whether you loved yourself, respected yourself, had a sense of integrity and were true to yourself? Would that give you a different perception about these events and their purpose? I know

A Rose Garden

it would. Then your focus would be on being true to yourself and allowing everything to happen as it may.

Exercise:

Write down five ways that you were not true to yourself in the last year. Write down what you would have done in those circumstances if you had been true to yourself. Pick the area in which you most want to be true to yourself and decide how you're going to handle the situation the next time it comes up. Write out a scenario for the situation and how you want to respond to it. Keep it with you at all times. Be sure your solution includes the actions you have to take to be true to yourself. Know that the outcome is perfect.

Affirmation:

By being true to myself, I set myself free.

Always Hope

"Man is, properly speaking, based upon hope. He has no other possession but hope; this world of his is emphatically the place of hope." Carlyle

When things get tough, we sometimes feel hopeless. We have a hard time believing that the future will be better than the present. Then we dwell on all of the problems we have in life and the shortages that exist in our lives today. Hopelessness is the most deadly disease. It destroys our lives and causes us to become depressed, which leads to physical sickness and a sense of uselessness. Like most diseases, there are varying degrees of severity, from mild cases to terminal ones. In the most severe cases, people focus on their situations, which intensifies their perceived severity. The effect is that they are then blinded to the possibilities that exist.

Let's take a look at what hope does and why it is as essential to life as air. When you hope, even when the physical evidence is totally to the contrary, you change your belief system, which changes your physiology and the chemical composition of your body. Then what you believe is possible changes, your actions change, and the results in your life change.

One of the things that cause us to give up is believing that the past is the sole predictor of the future. This is only true if you believe it to be true. Once again, that is your choice. The reason you are the way you are is because you have a belief that created your current situation. In order to change the future, you have to change the belief that created the situation. The future is totally dependent upon what you believe it will be. It doesn't have anything to do with the past. It is your choice.

A Rose Garden

When you believe the future cannot be different than the past, you give up your power.

Another reason is that you have limited beliefs about what you deserve, and thus you create situations that substantiate your beliefs. Your birthright is to share in all the abundance that the universe has to offer. In order to share in this infinite abundance, you must believe you deserve it! The sun shines on everyone. Abundance is available to all of us. It has nothing to do with what your skills or experiences are. Nothing! Thirdly, you have limited beliefs about how things are created. You believe that the future depends on having experience, education, being a certain age, having certain amounts of money, etc. Your belief system is limited to what you can see, feel and touch as well as what society has taught you about how things work. Some people believe that in order to make twice as much money, they have to work twice as long or twice as hard.

Some people must have physical evidence before they can hope that something can happen. Albert Einstein once said, "There are two ways to see life; everything is a miracle or nothing is a miracle." I choose to believe everything is a miracle. Then I can hope for an incredible future. I don't have to have any evidence for it to happen, and there don't have to be any qualifications (like age, education, amount of money) to hope you will have a miraculous future. Be careful with whom you share this incredible sense of hope. They may try to kill it, because they have restrictions about how things must happen.

When many of us were kids and we were asked what we wanted for our birthday, we didn't wonder where the money would come from to pay for those gifts. But we absolutely knew we would get them. You must have that same belief. Know it will happen. Release it to the universe, and let go of the need to figure out how. This knowing doesn't have to have any physical evidence in order for it to manifest itself. No matter what life looks like from a physical point of view, you know that the future will bring you what you want.

This sense of knowing will change your physiology. When you change your physiology, you change the energy you attract to yourself. In order for this to happen, you must focus on what you want to happen. Dismiss thoughts of impracticality based on a lack of physical evidence. Again, bring your focus back to what you are creating, not how it will be created. Continuously renew your sense of hope, and constantly release your need to control the outcome.

When you operate from a sense of knowing, regardless of the physical evidence to the contrary, your actions will change, your beliefs will change, and you will become a co-creator of your future!

Exercise:

In what area of your life are you having a hard time creating the outcomes you desire? What is your belief about this situation? What is the ideal scenario for this situation? What do you have to believe in order for this ideal situation to manifest itself? Keep a journal and write down all of the limiting thoughts and beliefs you have about this situation as they come into your mind. When you have a new limiting thought, add it to the list. When you see this thought coming up again, immediately dismiss it. Bring your attention back to what you want. Always look at where you want to go and who you want to be, not where you don't want to go or who you don't want to be.

Affirmation:

I am the person of my dreams. Everything happens for my highest good. I trust in the process of the universe.

A Rose Garden

Nobody Can Hurt Your Feelings Without Your Permission

"Reject your sense of injury and the injury itself disappears."
Marcus Aurelius

Feelings are subjective. They are not right or wrong; they are just yours. Anyone can say anything they want to you, and it is your choice whether or not your feelings get hurt. If I were to tell you that you were purple, you would probably just look at me like I was a nut. Why? Because you know that you're not purple! If I say something to you that you know isn't true, it can't hurt your feelings. The same thing holds true with everything else that people can say about you.

There are a couple of things that cause us to have our feelings hurt:

* Someone violates our values. If I were to tell you, "That was stupid," my conclusion is based on my values, not yours. There's no need for you to be insulted, because I said something that was a violation of my values, and I expressed myself in insensitive terms.

* We feel we are inadequate. Accept that you are who you are. Know absolutely that you do the very best that you can do with the resources you have available. Do not accept others' attempts to make you feel inadequate. You are never inadequate. Let's say I am the greatest writer in the world and have sold 50 million books. And let's say you come along and say, "I didn't like your latest book." That's okay. I know how good my book is, and I respect you enough to allow you to express your disagreement with me. But I refuse to have my feelings hurt by your point of view.

When we look at life this way, we take control and accept responsibility for ourselves, and we allow other people to express themselves without being brought into the emotional drama of the statement. Let go of the drama.

When your feelings get hurt, know that you gave your permission to have them hurt. Think about how you interpreted what was said or done, and then ask yourself how else you could have interpreted it. How many times do we assume the worst about things? This is another way we give our power away. Understand that it's the other person's problem and that he's just trying to unload his garbage in your life.

It's like guilt; you never have to accept it. Like a gift someone tries to give you, if you don't accept it, it still belongs to the giver. If you don't accept the insult, the insult still belongs to the giver.

Exercise:

Recall a time your feelings were hurt. Think of five other possible meanings behind what the other person did or said. Come up with a way that the event could be interpreted as a compliment.

Affirmation:

Whenever someone does something that could hurt my feelings, I will send him love.

A Rose Garden

You Have Exactly What You Believe You Deserve in Life

"The only thing that stands between a man and what he wants from life is often merely the will to try it and the faith to believe that it is possible." Richard M. De Vos

Most of us feel like we're victims of life and its circumstances. Our belief is that bad things happen to us because our parents didn't raise us right, we didn't get the right educational opportunities or the right job opportunities or career advancements, we got into the wrong relationship or we got in with the wrong group. Very few of us are willing to admit that we sabotage ourselves.

Let's look at this from God's point of view. God has an infinite supply of abundance that He pours into a master container. Every one of us chooses the size of the pipe that he connects to his master supply. There is an inexhaustible supply in this container, available to us twenty-four hours a day. The size of the pipe determines how much we get in our lives, and what we believe we deserve determines the size of the pipe. If we don't believe we deserve a lot, we attach a small pipe. It may be so small that hardly anything gets in, because we don't believe that we deserve it. God doesn't discriminate against us. He wants all of us to have everything we could possibly want. But in order to partake of life's abundance, we must believe we deserve it!

Look at some specific areas in your life. If you're a single woman, what kind of person and relationship do you believe you deserve? If we were to examine your relationships objectively, we would see that you attract a certain kind of person who reflects what you believe you deserve in a man. This type of man may abuse you physically, mentally or emotionally. This happens because you believe that you don't deserve to be treated like a queen! Do you find that whenever you get to a certain level of seriousness in a relationship, something happens and the two of you break up? If you are honest with yourself, you know that at a certain point, you get uncomfortable with the intimacy and then do or say something to ruin the relationship. Again, this is because you believe that that's all you deserve.

Look at the beliefs you have that cause you to sabotage those relationships. Ask how they serve you, even if it's in a negative way. You may have been emotionally scarred in a previous relationship, so you create a wall so the other person can only get so far. Now you must change your belief. You are not the person now that you were in the past. You must identify what you deserve in your relationships and stand up for it and don't settle for less.

Now look at your career. What's the most money that you've ever made in a year? What's the most you think you could make? Let's say you've made $100,000 in a year. Can you imagine making more than a $100,000 year? Do you think you could easily make a half-million dollars a year? Your answer reflects the belief you have about how much money you deserve. What are your beliefs about money? How have they served you? What must your beliefs about money be in order for you to attract an unlimited amount of it?

Go through this process for all of the areas of your life. Consider your health, finances, relationships, spiritual development, career, education, and personal growth.

Exercise:

Identify the area of your life where you feel the most deserving or feel that things usually go well. Look at what you believe about this area of your life. Maybe you believe that playing basketball comes easy

A Rose Garden

to you; it's fun to play, it challenges your body, it challenges your mind, and you love a challenge. Maybe you believe that you are unbeatable. Even when the other team outscores your team, you think you have won, because you have learned something about the skills of an opponent that you can incorporate into your game. So no matter what the outcome of the game, your belief is that you always win!

Now look at the area in which you believe you deserve the least. Let's say it is your belief about how much money you deserve to be paid. Your belief may be that your dad worked in a job where he only got a ten- or fifteen-cent-per-hour raise. You may believe that you can only climb the ladder one step at a time. You may believe you work your whole life trying to get a better job or a little bit more money or that you work for retirement. You may believe that life is a constant struggle, that nobody cares about you, that people are out to get you. Surely, you can see how this belief system would lead to minimal financial success.

Let's look at the difference between these two areas. In the basketball example, your belief is that everything flows easily and that you always win. In the other example, your belief is that you must struggle for every penny.

For every area of your life that you are struggling with, answer this question: "What must I believe in order for this area of my life to flow easily?" If you are struggling with your finances, say, "I deserve to have all the money I want and need to do everything that I could possibly desire to do. I deserve to have unlimited amounts come to me easily, effortlessly and continuously."

Affirmation:
I deserve the very best of all that life has to offer.

There Is Another Way to Look at This
(A Course in Miracles, Workbook, p. 50 1st edition p 50 2nd edition)

"It is impossible for a man to learn what he thinks he already knows."
Epictetus

Every event has many ways of being interpreted! Police officers who take eyewitness accounts of traffic accidents often say that accounts can differ so greatly that you would think different accidents were being described.

When life's events occur, we give them meaning based on our values, beliefs, life experiences and our mood at the time they occurred. Every human being has different values, beliefs and life experiences. The result is that every event is subject to different interpretations.

I used to drive 225 miles a day to make fourteen sales calls. I often got lost, which made me angry. Getting mad didn't help me find my way. Finally, I asked myself why I was getting lost. The answer was that I wasn't spending enough time looking up the directions. But I didn't like spending an hour every night getting directions. After I realized that the only way to solve my problem was to look up the directions, I took the time to do so every night, and I never got lost again. I found another way to look at the situation.

Let's take another example. Most people hate being in traffic jams. Next time you find yourself stuck in traffic, ask yourself, "How else can I look at this?" It can give you time to transition from work mode to mom or dad mode, or you can listen to audio tapes. Go to a magic shop and buy a red clown nose. When you get stuck in traffic, put the nose on and wave to the people next to you. Watch the expressions on their faces. You will have great fun, and you may even look forward to getting into traffic jams. You can also use the nose in bank or grocery

A Rose Garden

lines. Find a way to have fun, no matter what the situation is.

When you ask someone, "How are you?" the reply is often, "I'm having a bad day." Oh yeah? Having a bad day compared to what? The 200,000 people who die every day? Being a prisoner of war or a quadriplegic or living in rural Africa without electricity, plumbing or healthy food? How many people would love to be in your situation? Instead of asking people how they are, ask them about the best thing that has happened to them that day. You will help them see things another way.

When something unpleasant happens to us, our egos try to tell us how terrible our situations are. We may think, "Why is this happening to me? I don't deserve this. Why now? I don't have the money." You must find a way to stop this internal dialogue immediately and ask yourself how else you can look at the situation. As soon as you do, your mind will start asking different kinds of questions.

Let's say that your flight is delayed and your initial reaction is to get upset. Ask yourself how else you might look at the situation. You may decide, "I can read my book, which I am really enjoying. I can write a note to a friend. I can go to the gift shop. I can meditate or pray. I can make plans for the weekend. I can plan a surprise for my husband's birthday." You can take things one step further by planning in advance what you can bring with you to do if your flight gets delayed.

Remember the line from the Serenity Prayer, "God, grant me the Serenity to accept the things I cannot change..."? Situations that used to get you upset you can now accept with serenity. You can reclaim your power.

It is my belief that most of us want a sense of peace in our lives, no matter what is taking place on the outside. Looking at situations from a different perspective gives you that peace. Tell yourself, "This is happening for a reason. I may not understand why this is happening now, but I know that someday I will. Because I trust in God and the process of life, I will accept this situation without having to figure out why it is happening to me now."

The power of questions is that they change the way your mind processes external data and force you to look at situations differently.

Exercise:

What situation causes you to get upset most often? How else might you handle it in the future? Come up with at least ten different options and rank them in order, from the most appealing to the least appealing. Carry this list with you everywhere you go. When the situation comes up again, take the paper out and follow the instructions.

Affirmation:

Every time I get stuck, I will ask myself, "How else can I look at this?"

A Rose Garden

Have Faith in Yourself and Others

"Faith is the substance of things hoped for, the evidence of things not seen." Hebrews 11:1

Some of us find it easier to have faith in other people than we do in ourselves. Some of us have faith in ourselves, but we don't have faith in others. I find it easier to have faith in others, because I look for their admirable qualities. For some reason, I don't look for those qualities in myself.

We have all had experiences in which others have let us down or we have let ourselves down. Likewise, we have all had experiences in which others have come through for us and we have come through for ourselves. In other words, we have reasons for having faith in others and ourselves, or we have reasons for not having faith in others or ourselves.

We may measure faith by what we see externally, but regardless of what's going on externally, we shouldn't alter how we see ourselves or what we believe about ourselves. We use certain measuring sticks in our society, such as money, titles and material possessions. It's almost like we're playing Monopoly, and the more we have, the easier it is for us to have faith in ourselves. But you already have all the skills necessary to accomplish whatever you want in your life! Your job is to find these skills, develop them and use them. You must have faith that they're there.

For example, you have never questioned the existence of gravity, although you have absolute faith that it is there. You must have this same faith when it comes to knowing your unique gifts. Stop looking to other people to reinforce your identity and strengths. Look within yourself, be grateful for those all skills and strengths, know they're there, and then take them out and use them. As you do, your belief in yourself will grow.

Look deep within yourself and get in touch with who you are and what unique gifts you have. Then begin the process of expressing these gifts in the way you live your life. Know that you don't need external feedback to reinforce the fact that you have these gifts. You must know that they exist without someone else validating you. That's ego talking. Rather, you're looking for a sense of inner peace that comes from knowing you have a defined power and essence within you that you can plug into at any time. When you do, you can accomplish what you came here to accomplish.

Therefore, the faith you have is not necessarily manifested in what you do, but the faith is in knowing who you are. You are co-creator with God. Let go of the need to have a certain outcome. Do the work and allow God to create the outcome. Have the faith that you can do the work and that He will produce the outcome.

If you have a hard time having faith in others, look at them as if they're lost little children. Your first responsibility is to calm them down and let them know everything is okay. Let them know how much you appreciate them. Then look for the qualities in them that stand out. Tell them how much you appreciate them for their sincerity, compassion, insight or ability to listen.

Sometimes we have difficulty having faith in others, because it seems that whenever we do, we get disappointed. You are invited to let go of the past. Don't allow it to define who you are now. Give people the opportunity to prove to you that it was appropriate for you to have faith in them.

A Rose Garden

Exercise:

In which area of your life do you most want to have more faith in your abilities? Sit quietly in meditation and ask God to open your mind and heart to seeing where your skills and gifts are in this area. Meditate until it comes to you. Know that it will come. When you're ready to receive it, it will be there. Be like an expectant parent with tremendous anticipation of an upcoming birth. Don't have any trepidation. Just be excited about receiving the news of what your gifts are. Once you know them, develop a plan of action for using them. Know that the outside world will provide you with feedback on how you need to improve a particular skill or gift. Follow up on that feedback. Change your skills, review them, revise them, refine them and perfect them.

Affirmation:

I have complete faith in myself, in God and in e
veryone else in my life.

What I Love About Myself

"For all true love is grounded on esteem." George Villiers

Knowing what you love about yourself should be an easy lesson to learn. For most of us it isn't, because we aren't taught how to love ourselves. We are taught that it is important to be humble and that extolling one's virtues isn't humble. Consequently, we have learned to accept the criticisms that others have of us. Because we integrate these beliefs into our sense of self, we don't focus much energy on what we love about ourselves. And because we are not taught to appreciate our gifts and talents, we haven't identified what we love about ourselves.

I believe learning to love ourselves is the first thing we have to do in order to live happy and successful lives. It is absolutely necessary if we want this life to be one of significant growth. Some say that loving God comes first. I think if loving ourselves comes first, then we look to God with totally open minds, hearts and spirits.

How do we learn to love ourselves? If we see ourselves as physical extensions of God in a physical body, we can embrace our divinity. If we accept ourselves as divine beings, we focus on the love aspect of life.

Another aspect of loving ourselves is accepting ourselves just the way we are. We live in a world of duality: hot and cold, in and out, up and down, etc. Everything has an opposite, and since we were taught to be humble, we tend to put ourselves on the negative sides of these dualistic comparisons. My challenge to you is to let go of all of these comparisons and accept yourself as a perfect divine extension of God. In this perfection, it is acceptable to love yourself! This love is an expression of the reuniting of yourself with your creator. This will empower you to live a life expressing this God force.

A Rose Garden

By loving yourself, you can reach out to love everyone around you. By learning to accept yourself exactly as you are, it is easier to accept others as they are.

Also, you can now accept your life plan as a perfect expression of God through you.

You accept all of the events in your life as perfect lessons given to you so that you might learn who you are and how to express yourself fully and completely in human form. Nothing is good or bad, right or wrong; it just is.

Exercise:

Develop a list of things you love about yourself. How do you express those things in your life? How do you impact other people? Remember that you are creating a legacy.

Affirmation:

I am grateful for the gifts that have been given to me, and I share these gifts with everyone with whom I come in contact.

The Value of Wisdom

"By three methods we may learn wisdom: First, by reflection, which is noblest; second, by imitation, which is the easiest; and third, by experience, which is the bitterest." Confucius

When we're young, we rarely see the value of wisdom. As we get older, it seems as if our life experiences teach us more and more about wisdom. The dictionary defines wisdom as "an understanding of what is true, right or lasting, common sense, sagacity, or good judgment." I think my definition of wisdom would be "common sense." How do we access our common sense and use it? By creating a gap of time between events and our responses to them. So often, we simply react. But wisdom enables us to use the most appropriate response to a situation, considering all the factors involved, and it allows us to take the action that creates the best outcome for all involved.

Learning the value of wisdom involves two steps. The first is to get wisdom and use it in our own lives, and the second part is to teach wisdom to others. Wisdom enables us to make better decisions for everyone involved. Therefore, when we use wisdom we are raising the consciousness of humankind. That is why it is so important to teach wisdom to others.

Find someone who exhibits the qualities you want, and read everything you can about him or her. If possible, arrange to interview this person. There are laws of life that work, no matter who uses them. All you have to do is to find out which laws this person is using and use them yourself.

You can also gain wisdom through meditation. Ask for an understanding of a particular issue in your life, and then meditate on

A Rose Garden

the issue until the answer comes. Also look for the answer to appear in an everyday experience. In the movie *Field of Dreams*, the main character was told by a mysterious voice, "Build it and they will come." With wisdom, the applicable saying is, "Ask and you shall receive." Believe, have faith, expect the answer, and wait for it to appear.

Wisdom enables you to experience life more fully, more richly and more deeply. We have chosen to live in our bodies, so what could be more fulfilling than living the fullest and richest lives possible? This can be done if you pursue wisdom, and when you receive this gift, share it with everyone you meet. Together, we will raise the consciousness of humanity!

Exercise:

Commit to consciously searching for wisdom in your life in whatever way instinctively comes to you.

Affirmation:

I cherish the wisdom that is available to me from every human and divine being that has ever existed. I ask them to share their wisdom with me, and I thank them for their gift of wisdom. I share my wisdom with whoever wishes to receive it.

Live Life One Hundred Percent

"This body is not a home, but an inn; and only for a short time."
Lucius Annaeus Seneca

One of the most important lessons we can learn in our lives is that it isn't how many years we live that matters; it's what we do with those years. The only thing we're guaranteed is the present moment. Not one of us knows the time of his death. What's important is what we do with the time we have available to us. If you truly know you have a limited amount of time to accomplish what you want with your life, then what you do and how you spend your time will be affected by that knowledge. The most important thing you can do is fully participate in the game of life. No matter what life gives to you, your responsibility is to make the most of it.

On a scale of one to ten, how fully are you living your life? What is it going to take for you to live more fully? How you live is based on your beliefs about life. If you believe taking risks is dangerous, you will play things safe. Your fears will dictate how you lead your life. This may minimize your failures and disappointments, but it will also deprive you of the opportunity to achieve great things. In order to grow and become what you have the ability to become, it's necessary to take chances.

Some people are afraid to fail. But if you change your definition of failure, you will change the way you live. For example, if you say, "The only way I can fail is if I don't try," then whenever you try, you will be a success.

Terry Cole Whitaker's book *What You Think of Me is None of My Business* had a tremendous impact on me when I first started

A Rose Garden

my professional speaking career. I would get in front of an audience of several hundred people and worry about what they were going to think about me. There was no way that I could know what anyone expected of me. The only way for me to give a dynamic presentation was to be myself and give them permission to think of me whatever they wanted to think. Be yourself, live life full out, and let others think what they want about you. They will anyway.

How often do you do things because of your concern about what other people will think of you? How does this compromise your integrity as a human being? A lot of people live in fear of controversy or hurting other people's feelings. But when we live only to please others, we compromise ourselves. When this happens, we miss out on living life fully. When you look back on your life, one of the most important things you will evaluate, in terms of the success, is how true you were to yourself. If you fast forward to the last day of your life and look back, you will regret all the things you didn't do.

Make a list of all the things you want to do before your life is over. Post the list on the bathroom mirror or in front of the toilet or carry a copy in your pocket. Make the completion of this list one of your highest life priorities.

No matter what your beliefs are, it is absolutely essential that you put all of your energy into your life. All of us have room to improve when it comes to living more fully. You deserve to live the fullest and richest life possible, and you deserve to share the benefits of a full life.

Exercise:

Think of three areas of your life that you would like to live more fully. Write down three things that you would do in each area to enable yourself to live more fully. Share this list with your best friend and ask him or her to be encouraging and to engage you in reaching your goal. Ask him or her to be your coach and cheerleader.

Affirmation:

I love life, and I live my life fully and without regard for other people's opinions.

A Rose Garden

It's the Quality of the Years You Live That Matters Not the Quantity

"As is a tale, so is life: not how long it is but how good it is, is what matters." Lucius Annaeus Seneca

For some reason in our society, we believe that the most important thing in life is how many years you live, not the quality of life you have in those years. When a twenty-year-old dies, it's considered a tragedy. It's sad when an eighty-year-old dies, but we at least say he or she lived a full life.

I believe it isn't important how old you are when you die. What is important is what you've done in the years that you've been alive. In 1991, basketball star "Magic" Johnson, at age thirty-two, was diagnosed positive for the HIV virus. Even if he had died back then, he still would have lived more life than most people who lived to be eighty-two—because all of the things he did and the intensity with which he did them.

If a person has been in sales for twenty-five years, he is asked if he has had twenty-five years' experience as a salesman or one year that's been repeated twenty-five times. In your life, are you continuously growing, or are you repeating the experiences of yesterday, last week, last month or last year? There's a saying, attributed to business visionary Ray Krok, "We are either green and growing or ripe and rotting." Which are you?

If you knew that this was the last year of your life, what would you do differently? Let's assume you still have to work. Would you stop watching television? Whom would you call to mend a relationship? Would the things that are important to you now still be important?

With whom would you spend your time? Would you be more tolerant? More patient? More accepting? More forgiving?

Has anyone you've known died while the two of you were in the middle of a strained relationship? Did you feel a deep sense of regret at not having resolved the issue? Life is about relationships—with yourself, with God, with your spouse, your children, everyone. If you are constantly striving to build these relationships, then it won't matter how long you live. You will die happy, because you did everything you could to live a good and full life. Talk to a person who has been given a terminal diagnosis and ask him how the experience changed his life.

Exercise:

Pick one area of your life that you would like to focus more attention on. Maybe you want to take piano lessons, learn how to use a computer, exercise or volunteer at a nursing home. Maybe you want to repair a damaged relationship or build a new one. Embrace that area fully and sink yourself into it. Focus on it. Give it all of your attention, all of your energy. I guarantee that you will feel more alive and more complete. Be an active participant in life, not an observer.

Make a list of all the things you want to do before you die. Post that list on the refrigerator or on your mirror. Keep it in your car, and use it as your road map to lead your life. Live in such a way that if you were to die today, you wouldn't have any regrets.

Affirmation:

I live my life with the intensity that I would live it with the knowledge that this was the last year of my life.

A Rose Garden

Part 6

Spiritual Beliefs That Will Create More Powerful and Meaningful Relationships

A Rose Garden

The Golden Rule

"The best thing about giving of ourselves is that what we get is always better than what we give. The reaction is greater than the action."
Orson Swett Marden

Most of us learned The Golden Rule early in life: "Do unto others as you would have others do unto you." We know this means that we should treat other people the same way we want them to treat us. This has also been expressed as, "What goes around comes around," "What you give out, you get back," "You reap what you sow," "Turnaround is fair play" and "Getting your just desserts."

We would drastically change the world if we would treat other people the same way we want them to treat us! We must be the example. Begin by asking yourself if the way you are treating other people is the way you want them to treat you. For people who don't have good images of themselves, the issue is exactly the reverse: Would you treat others the way you treat yourself?

We must see ourselves as valuable individuals, regardless of our behavior, looks, financial status or job title. We are physical extensions of our divine creator, and as such, we are divine beings! We are growing into our divinity as we are living our lives. We are learning who we really are. Therefore, our value is in who we are, not what we do. Our challenge is to see everyone for who they really are, not for what they do. Treat everyone with reverence and respect, even if they don't believe they deserve it. Believe in them long enough and they will start to believe in themselves.

Somehow we forget that although there are six billion humans on this planet, we make up one human body and form a collective human consciousness. One of our purposes in life is to help to raise the collective consciousness of humankind. Look for and find the good and beauty in every person and situation you encounter.

We are not our bodies. We have temporarily taken up residence in these bodies, but like our homes, they are just temporary residences. As one, we are manifested as different aspects of the one divine being. If we look for God in everyone, we will find Him. Treat others like God, because they are the same aspect of God as you are. Then we will treat everyone as if we just met God! Once all of us do that, we cease needing to exist in our physical bodies, because we have discovered our true identities and lived them and become them.

When you encounter an angry person, it's easy to get pulled into their anger and return it. But what if you choose to see her as a frightened child and return her anger with love? You don't have to hug her or kiss her but send your love to her from your heart. When people come to you with anything but love, they are asking you to love them. At that moment, they don't believe that they are worthy of being loved, because they aren't saying or doing things they consider lovable. They have lost sight of the fact that love isn't dependent upon behavior. However, love is given freely as a gift, without any strings or attachments.

When someone comes to you in love, it is easy to recognize him as a part of God, receive his love and return it. But when his contrary ego presents you with anger, hostility, resentment or stubbornness, it is usually impossible to see God in him. Instead, you respond to his behavior with your own brand of anger. It becomes a competition. Your challenge is to learn to recognize that his ego is present and that its only job in life is to create and maintain chaos. You need to find the spirit or the higher self in every situation you are in. The spirit's job is

A Rose Garden

to create and maintain peace!

Return everything that is presented to you with love! When I am upset or hurt, the thing I want most is to be loved, but my ego gains control and tries to make it impossible for my spirit to rise. In other words, when I need to be loved the most is when I make it the hardest for anyone to love me. The same is true for most people.

Exercise:

Observe someone who is upset (assuming you aren't involved in the situation). Notice how her ego takes control. Look for God within her. Know that God is there and send your love to God, not to this person's behavior. Hold that sacred aspect of God in your heart, surround it in golden light and then release it in love. Practice this with as many people as you can. When you see your ego acting out, you are now ready for the ultimate test. Send love to yourself and envelop yourself in golden light. Magically, you will see the ego leave, and your higher self will appear.

Affirmation:

I look for and find God in everyone I meet. The beauty of God shines everywhere.

You're Never Alone

"If you knew who walks beside you and the way you have chosen, fear would be impossible."
(*A Course in Miracles,* Text, p. 353 1st edition, p. 378 2nd edition)

Sometimes it's impossible for us to understand that we're never alone, that there is someone there to guide us, to help us, to instruct us, to comfort us, to love us. Why is that hard for us to comprehend? Because we only believe in what we can relate to using our five senses. We're taught to be critics and skeptics. The prevailing mindset is that if you can't scientifically prove something's existence, it doesn't exist. That is one way to perceive life.

Another perception is that we are loved unconditionally. Who loves us? You can call it a spiritual guide, an angel, God, higher self or whatever works for you. How do you find that entity? The answer is simple. Get quiet and ask, "Where are you? Are in you inside of me, in front of me, beside me, behind me, above or below me? Talk to me, please." Then listen carefully, because what that being has to say may be said softly or quietly. It may require you to be very sensitive, aware and non-judgmental.

You can handle anything knowing that you have a spiritual guide with unlimited strength, wisdom, knowledge and love. Your spiritual guide is there to support you, so be open to its help. Acknowledge it, thank it and be grateful for it. Play with it, have fun with it and enjoy having it in your life. Don't be afraid of it.

We all have mentors. Some of them are physical, and some of them are spiritual. Your physical teachers can be brought to you in an instant, and their wisdom, guidance and knowledge are yours for the asking.

A Rose Garden

Likewise, spiritual beings are with you and around you all the time. Talk to people who see them. They are never alone. They are always in a crowd. My friend Rijckie sees spirit guides everywhere she goes. Sometimes spirit guides are so real to her that she can't distinguish them from the people with physical bodies!

Exercise:

Go to your favorite place, sit, meditate and ask who is there. Ask it for its name and ask it for the role that it plays in your life. Ask it what it needs to tell you. When it leaves, embrace it and thank it. Ask it how you can best use the gifts it gives you.

Affirmation:

I am always surrounded by loving beings and loving light, and I am always safe.

Treat Your Body as a Sacred Temple

"This body, full of faults, has yet one great quality: Whatever it encounters in this temporal life depends upon one's actions." Nagrjuna

We all have bodies, but how many of us like the ones we have? Unfortunately, we live in a society with a Madison Avenue mentality. All the models are skinny, and the men are very muscular, and they are all in their twenties. We think that's what we should look like, but even when these models are interviewed, they never seem to be happy with their own bodies!

I believe we choose our bodies before we come into this world. We choose the attributes that will enable us to learn the lessons we come here to learn. I have a friend who was bitten by a tick in a Japanese prisoner-of-war camp in World War II and suffered permanent damage to one of her legs. I asked her why she believed this happened, and she said that having a gimpy leg has enabled her to relate on the human level. Without it, life would have been too easy for her. Incidentally, she has walked with crutches since she was two years old, but one of her life dreams is to wear high heels and dance for a day!

Embrace the body you have and see it as a sacred temple. Treat it with love and respect. It is the vehicle that you have to take you through this lifetime. Love your body and honor it. Treat your body the way you would treat your best friend in the world.

Feed it with foods that energize you. Exercise in a way that you enjoy. There are stresses in your everyday life, so it is vital that you nurture your body when you get stressed. Maintain a balance between your personal and professional lives. We work to live, not live to work. We all know people who are workaholics. You need to enjoy the fruits

A Rose Garden

of your labor. Think of your body as your partner. It will enable you to live the kind of life you want to live. Don't abuse your body so badly that you have a heart attack or stroke or get some other debilitating disease. Embrace your body, love it, thank it, and be grateful to it for all that it gives you.

Exercise:

Make a list of the things you do not like about your body. List five reasons to love that aspect of your body just the way it is. Take time to thank each of your organs for all the incredible work it has done to provide you with the quality of life you have. Take time to see how incredibly rich you are. You can see, hear, walk and speak. Many people would give anything to be able to do those things. Develop an attitude of gratitude toward your body.

Affirmation:

I love my body. It is the sacred temple I have chosen to get me through this life.

Your Most Important Relationship Is the One With Yourself

"All men are alike in their lower natures; it's in their higher characters that they differ." Christian N. Bovee

Some people believe that the most important relationship in life is with God. My belief is that our relationships with God are enhanced when we start with great relationships with ourselves. By cultivating the relationship with yourself, you build a strong, solid foundation. You are open to learning about and receiving the magnificent nature of your creator.

The goal of building the relationship with yourself is to learn to love yourself unconditionally. There are many ways to learn to love yourself unconditionally. Begin by journaling every day. In one section, have a place to compliment yourself. Make sure you find something to compliment yourself about every day. Set up sections where you record all the things you like and love about yourself.

Make sure you journal every day, especially when you are feeling depressed. On these days, not only should you journal but you must also read what you have written. This is important, because that part of yourself that doesn't see your value is occupying your mind when you are feeling down. But that part of yourself that is blind to your value cannot exist when it is showered with compliments. It's like bringing a snowman into the house; it will melt.

The value of this practice is that it helps balance our lives. We spend an inordinate amount of time and energy criticizing our performances and ourselves. Balance that by taking time to nurture yourself and really seeing both your inner and outer beauty. This isn't egotistical. It

A Rose Garden

is taking the time to admire the gifts given to you by your creator.

An extraordinary way to build your relationship with yourself is to stop criticizing yourself. Be gentle and loving with yourself. Handle yourself as if you were the most beautiful and loved person ever created! You are. Embrace yourself as an incredible extension of God. God is within you, within every single cell in your body, within every thought you have, within every action you take. He loves you more than you'll ever know. Know the gentleness and expansiveness of this love and accept it as unconditional. Your God loves you, no matter what you say or do. You volunteered to come here and experience that in this physical world. Focus your mind, heart and attention on having this experience of God in your body. Every relationship requires cultivation in order to grow. Therefore, you must take action to cultivate the relationship you have with yourself.

Understand that by doing this you become whole. As a whole spiritual being who nurtures and loves himself, you can now reach out to everyone in your life. You may start with God and then reach out to your spouse, children, siblings, parents, friends, boss, peers and subordinates. You are now prepared to enter into these relationships from a place of fullness and completeness.

Enjoy your commitment to loving yourself and seeing yourself as the most important relationship you have in the world. And on behalf of everyone whose lives you touch, I thank you for caring about yourself and taking care of yourself.

Exercise:

Journal every day. Write down self-compliments, things you like about yourself and things you love about yourself. It's okay to repeat these things. Repetition reprograms your mind to believe what you're saying. After thirty days of journaling, review your notes and identify one area you define as something you like about yourself. Write about it as if you were your own best friend and that you were writing a letter to a person you would like to meet you. Describe yourself in glowing terms. Don't be shy. This is about beginning a process of accepting your inheritance as a divine being. After you have written this, sit in front of a mirror and read it out loud to yourself. Look deep inside yourself and think about what you feel.

Affirmation:

I love myself.

A Rose Garden

The Power of Prayer

"I could be whatever I wanted to be if I trusted that music, that song, that vibration of God that was inside of me." Shirley MacLaine

Prayer is defined as talking to God. Meditation is defined as listening to God. One of your challenges is to talk to God in prayer like He is your most trusted friend, the person with whom you can be totally free to say anything you want to say. You will never be judged, condemned or criticized. He loves you enough to allow you the freedom to do what you want. He's always with you and always listening. When you talk to God in prayer, tell Him what you want.

Scientists have conducted medical studies of patients who were prayed for without their knowledge. The studies show that people who have been prayed for have been cured faster, with less pain and fewer complications. If prayer isn't an intricate part of your life, allow it to be. Pray and release your problems and concerns to God. Put them in a bag, give them to Him, and let go. Release your worries and concerns to Him daily. Pray to Him for wisdom, insight, truth and the solution to the challenges that you are dealing with. Thank Him for the lessons that He's bringing to you, knowing that the events you're experiencing are co-created by the two of you, with God having the knowledge of the best way to teach you the lesson. Ask Him that there may be an easier, less painful way to learn it, and always surrender to the fact that He knows best. Ask to be comforted as you move through troubles. Ask Him for the courage to go into the pain and see the beauty in it. Ask to see the lesson, the love and the wisdom that is being sent to you. Ask for the strength to embrace the event, no matter how painful it appears to be, and to know that the pain will pass.

There are many things we do in our lives that are rituals. We brush our teeth, bathe, eat and sleep. Make prayer a daily ritual. Designate a special place to pray, and if you can't pray in your sacred spot, know that you can pray anywhere. The important thing isn't where you do it; it's just important that you do it.

Exercise:

List your daily prayer requests in your journal. Once a month, spend a few minutes reviewing these requests to see how many of them were answered. Thank God for answering your prayers. There's nothing more powerful than a grateful heart. There's nothing that will give more, bring more or create more than a constant sense of gratitude for everything that you have, everything you are and everything that happens in your life.

Affirmation:

I pray every single day of my life.

A Rose Garden

Give Love

"Love is the essence of God." Ralph Waldo Emerson

After seeing several of my presentations, a psychologist once told me that each of my talks should stand on its own with a separate theme but that all of my talks bore a central theme—love! Actually, I was thrilled. To me, it's all about love, so I felt I was getting my point across.

We learned as babies that we would receive love when we did things of which our parents approved. Love was a reward for good behavior. As adults, we give and withhold love based on the same criteria. If someone does or says something we approve of, we give him our love. If he says or does something we disapprove of, often we withhold our love. Sometimes we are even nasty about it. By having these rigid criteria for giving love, we create a lot of pain for others. They return the favor by giving and withholding their love.

It is my belief that all of us want people to love us, no matter what we say or do. Their love is like food; we hunger for it. The only way to ensure that you get all the love you want is to give your love to everyone, no matter what they say or do! This is unconditional love, which means loving others regardless of what they say or do. Conditional love judges behavior and gives love only if the behavior is acceptable. Unconditional love does not judge, and it has no connection to behavior. This does not mean that we should condone unacceptable behavior; it means that we shouldn't withhold love when there is unacceptable behavior.

Unconditional love is a real challenge to give. One way is to invoke Nike's old slogan, "Just Do It." Become aware of when you are withholding your love. This means you must constantly ask yourself two questions: "Is this a loving act?" and "Are these loving words?" Be aware of how you feel when you are doing or saying something loving. Where in your body do you feel it? When you become aware of this feeling, you will realize how much you like it and will do it more often. Conversely, become aware of how it feels when you do or say something nasty. Where do you feel that? Become aware of that feeling and know that you want to avoid it. Also become aware of how you feel when someone else says or does something to you that is hurtful. If you don't like that feeling, then they won't either. Just as we like to be around people who make us feel good about ourselves, others like to be around people who make them feel good about themselves.

We all want to be loved for who we are, not what we do. All of us do things we wish we could take back. We don't want to be judged for those things. The challenge is to stop judging yourself, others and all the events in your life.

Exercise:

Recall a specific time when you were loving toward someone. Get in touch with the feelings you experienced. Relive the experience over and over. Intensify the feelings. How did the other person feel? Now remember a time when you were nasty to someone. How did that make you feel? Get in touch with those feelings. Which way would you rather feel? Remember that it is your choice. Look at the power you have when you are always giving love.

Affirmation:

I have an infinite amount of love to give away and don't have much time to give it away.

A Rose Garden

Let Go, Let God

"God grant me the serenity to accept the things I cannot change, the courage to change the things I can, and the wisdom to know the difference." Reinhold Niebuhr

My favorite prayer is "Let go, let God." But I still struggle with this lesson. I understand the intellectual principle, which is to surrender life to God and know that everything that happens is perfect. Nevertheless, I do things to try to control outcomes.

Once it occurred to me that I could make God my chief financial officer. If you were to hire a chief financial officer, you would tell him what his duties were and then let him do his job! You wouldn't keep going into his office and micromanaging his every task. No, you would trust your CFO to do his job. And in this case, no one can be trusted to do a job more than God!

When you ask God to do something, He will do it. All you have to do is let go. Relinquish the need to control the outcome, because you know God's skill is beyond your wildest comprehension. If we accept that everything that happens to us is for our good, then we can simply say the prayer, ask for what we want and let it go. We no longer have the need to control the outcome, because we know it is for our highest good. As always, the choice is yours, but let God carry your burdens for you. Trust that true power is surrendering all the outcomes to God.

Outcomes have nothing to do with our purpose. We are spiritual beings who have gladly and happily accepted the assignment to experience God in human form. It should be easy to let go of our human shortcomings. They teach us about life's negative energy.

Now let go. Experience life and all of its positive energies and all of its miraculous opportunities so that you can make quantum leaps in understanding, learning, relationships, love and a limitless concept of life. What do we need to do to make this happen? Simply let go. Let God.

Exercise:

Identify something you're ready to let go of and give it to God. Do it in your favorite spot, in your meditative state, surrounded by God's presence. It's all around you, and its beauty is beyond anything that words can describe. You greet each other and God says to you, "What can I do for you?" You say, "God, I'm scared. I don't know how to let go of things down here or how to let You handle everything." Listen to His response. When you're finished this time, you have a gift for God. That gift is the complete surrender of the outcomes in every area of your life. Look at the smile on God's face, feel what God is feeling, and know that you have just reconnected with your creator, with your supreme being. His gratitude for you expressing yourself as His friend overwhelms you emotionally, and you now feel the presence of God in ever cell of your body. Get in touch with that feeling. Experience and know that it is there for you every second of your life.

Affirmation:

I experience the ecstasy of letting go and letting God.

A Rose Garden

Trust Your Creator

"The best proof of love is trust." Dr. Joyce Brothers

Although we may think we trust God, our actions often don't support that. When our lives are falling apart, we pray, "God, please fix my life." When things are going better, our actions effectively say, "Okay, I'll take back control of my life now." How would your life be different if you believed that before you were born, you and God developed a plan for your life as a physical means of experiencing Him in this world?

When you pray for God's help, talk to Him as if He were the best friend you've ever had and as if you could say anything to Him. We can tell Him we're scared, angry, confused, frustrated and frightened. You can say, "God, I need your help. Please help me to understand what my role is here. What is the purpose of this circumstance in my life? I would appreciate if you would help it pass quickly."

Talk to God every day, all day. When you're driving, turn the radio off in the car and talk to God instead. If you're scared, tell Him that. Tell Him you really want to trust Him and that you don't know how. Ask for guidance, and then be acutely aware of everything in your life as the guidance you're asking for. Our lives are much happier, more peaceful, more loving and more content when we rely on God. I spend most of my time in my head intellectualizing and analyzing everything. My challenge is to be in my heart and to know God is with me all the time and that He is always working through me.

A major factor in trusting God is to acknowledge that He is master teacher and that He brings events into your life in perfect order and timing to present to you the experiences that will enable you to learn.

When you trust your teacher, you don't question the lessons; you just do the work. Some of the lessons are joyful, easy and fun. Some of them are extraordinarily painful. When you're in the painful lessons, it's very important that you trust what you can't see. If you're blind and I reach my hand out to grasp your hand, you'd better trust that I'm going to take you to safety. Reach your hand out, feel God taking a hold of it and know that he'll lead you to safety.

Exercise:

Identify one area of your life where you're having a difficult time surrendering to God. Write God a letter, telling Him exactly what you want in every detail. Tell Him why you don't believe that you deserve to get what you want. Ask Him to remove these fears and instill in you the absolute knowing that you deserve all that He has to give to you. Observe the results.

Affirmation:

Thank you, God, for teaching me to trust you.

A Rose Garden

Someday You Will Understand

"All of our knowledge has its origin in our perceptions."
Leonardo da Vinci

At some point in our childhoods, our parents said to us, "Someday you will understand." Don't you think that God says this to us all the time? We don't understand the big picture and how our life experiences fit into it. We function at the level of the five senses and find activity outside of the five senses hard to understand. Often, we fail to see how unpleasant events fit into our life's purpose. Maybe you lost a job, and you don't understand why you got fired. God says that someday you will understand.

On September 25, 1966, I was walking in downtown Dubuque, Iowa, with the woman that I wanted to marry. The next thing I knew, I woke up in a hospital, having suffered a grand mal seizure. I was working my way through college, and when I went back to work, I was fired. I had to drop out of school. I moved back to Chicago, and the girl I loved started dating somebody else. All of this seemed like a tragedy. One day I was perfectly healthy, going to school and in love, and the next thing I knew, I was out of work, out of school and alone. Life looked totally bleak.

But because of the grand mal seizure, I was deferred from the army and didn't have to go to Viet Nam, and a year later, I met the woman I've been married to for the past thirty-seven years. The seizure, which seemed like a tragedy at the time, was clearing the way for me to meet my wife. We don't understand some of the things that happen to us in this lifetime.

When we trust God, we accept the fact that someday we'll

understand what happened to us. I think of God as the great maestro in the orchestra, each one of us having his own instrument and own music to play. We trust the maestro to bring all of our music together to make a great concert. All we have to do is our part. We don't have to know the outcome. What we do have to do is trust and know that someday we'll understand what all of our lives were about.

In the process of trusting and relinquishing the need to understand, we can go to that place where we all know intuitively and instinctively that we can become more than what we are. With that knowing, we can reach within and tap into the resources that are available to us to propel us to the levels that we can reach.

Exercise:

Identify three times in your life when you didn't understand why a particular event happened. Relinquish those events to God and thank Him for bringing them to you. Say, "I know that someday I will understand."

Affirmation:

I trust God, and I release my need to understand the purpose of the events in my life.

A Rose Garden

Ask Better Questions

"The quality of your life is dependent upon the quality of your questions." Anthony Robbins

Our internal dialogue is nothing more than a series of questions. If something goes wrong, we may ask, "Why me, God? Why now?" You may say things like, "I don't deserve for this to happen to me. This is terrible." These are all negative thoughts, and since we know that our thoughts create our future, we logically know then that negative thoughts create a negative future. But most of the time, we don't accept responsibility for controlling our thoughts.

In order to live a happier, more fulfilling and satisfying life, you must ask yourself better questions. Ask questions that are productive: What do I have to believe about this situation to be successful? What do I have to do to change this? What are my options? What is the best thing that could happen in this situation? How did I create this? What would I want instead of this? What is this event teaching me? How can I have fun with this? What would be another way to look at this?

Exercise:

Develop a list of questions that you consider productive in changing your perception or point of view about a specific event. Come up with a list of five to ten questions to ask yourself about this event, and carry it around with you. When you find yourself feeling upset or angry, ask yourself these questions. Observe how your physiology changes and how the situation changes.

Affirmation:

I always ask powerful questions.

There is a Silver Lining in Every Cloud*

"Success is to be measured not so much by the position one has reached in life as by the obstacles which he has overcome to succeed."
Booker T. Washington

A good friend of mine, W. Mitchell, lives his life according to the saying, "It's not what happens to you that matters; it's what you do about it." W. Mitchell was driving his motorcycle when a laundry truck sideswiped it, igniting his gas tank and giving him third-degree burns over eighty percent of his body. He had fifteen skin graft operations and had all ten fingers amputated.

Another time, he was flying in an airplane that wasn't properly deiced. The plane crashed, severing his spine. In the hospital, he was feeling sorry for himself because he could no longer do so many of the things that he used to be able to do. Then he realized that he needed to focus on what he could do, not on what he couldn't do. From there, he went on to become a very successful professional speaker.

Someone else who sees the positive side is Captain Gerald Coffee, who was a prisoner of war in Vietnam for seven and a half years. When he was captured, he said the experience was going to give him an opportunity to get to know himself and his God better.

Many people would consider both of these real-life examples to be tragedies. But both of these men made their lives and their careers because of how they handled difficult circumstances. The key is to find the lesson in everything that happens. For something good to result from a particular event, your responsibility is to find the silver lining. To do that, ask yourself, "What can I learn from this?"

I once had a job selling magnetic mattress pads, and things just

A Rose Garden

weren't working out. A friend asked, "What is the lesson here for you to learn?" My response: "To follow my instinct." In the initial interview, all they had asked me to do was memorize a thirty-page script and get to work. I knew that something wasn't right, because they weren't interested in my personality or my skills. The second lesson was not to make a decision from a place of desperation. I had been having cash flow problems and saw this job as a quick fix to the situation. The third lesson was that it gave me the confidence in my ability to memorize a significant amount of material, deliver it and instill my personality in the presentation.

Part of me wanted to blame the company for being irresponsible, unorganized and unethical. My higher self said, "I created this situation to learn something. I absolutely believe that everything that happens in my life is because I brought it into my life to learn from it."

Whatever is happening to you in life, always look for the silver lining. Always look for the pearl. Always look for the good and the beauty in everything and everyone that you come in touch with. You will find what you're looking for.

Exercise:

Identify one event in your life that you consider to be a tragedy. Ask yourself what lesson can be learned from the experience. Come up with at least five answers. If the event is so painful you have a difficult time coming up with answers, visualize yourself in a theater watching the event playing on a movie screen. If that is still too painful, see yourself moving up to the balcony of the theater. What you're doing is removing yourself further and further from the emotional pain of the event, which will enable you to find the lesson.

Affirmation:

I trust that everything that happens in my life is for my highest good. I am always looking for the lesson from every event.

(Footnotes)
* Quoted from Ann Mazer

A Rose Garden

There is More to Life Than What We Experience With Our Five Senses

"Beyond the senses are their objects, and beyond the objects is the mind. Beyond the mind is pure reason, and beyond reason is the Spirit in man. Beyond the Spirit in man is the Spirit of the universe, and beyond is the Spirit Supreme." Upanishads

Most people's experience of life is limited to the things they can see, hear, smell, touch and taste. So when we relate to something that is not experienced through the use of one of the senses, we can sometimes be critical and deny its existence.

I am referring to is the spiritual or non-physical realm: God, your higher self, angels, spirit guides, past-life regression, channeling, seeing auras, reading energy, intuitiveness, psychic energy, etc. Learning to develop any of these skills is like learning anything else; you need a teacher, and you need to practice.

In the following exercise, we are going to discuss how to access spiritual beings to guide you in your life's journey. Our challenge is to learn to move beyond the five senses and move to where the sacred parts of ourselves exist, where our higher selves wait for us quietly to come visit.

Exercise:

Go into your meditative state or go to your favorite place in the world. This place can be real or it can be imagined. Use your five senses to identify every detail. Smell the air and the flowers. If you're near water, hear the sounds. If you're outside, hear the wind as it goes through the trees. Capture this in every detail. Intensify the colors you see. Invite anyone you want to your party: God, Jesus, Buddha, great figures in history, friends or family members who have transitioned. Invite all of them to sit with you in a circle. This is your party; they have come to honor you. Each one of them comes up to you to tell you what he or she loves and admires about you. When they're finished, they come to you a second time and tell you what you need to know for your highest good. Each one comes to you with a gift. Honor that person by opening the gift in front of him and telling him how you'll use it to make your life more complete. If you're not sure how you will use the gift, ask him how he thinks you should use the gift. When everyone is finished, stand and give thanks for the infinite love that exists. Hug them as they leave. Then they will tell you they will always be there for you. Call them when you want them, and they will be there to answer. After they've all left, slowly come back into your environment, knowing that you can go back any time.

Affirmation:

I thank God for teaching me how to get in touch with Him and all the higher beings that reside within me.

A Rose Garden

Life is Sacred

"The best and most beautiful things in the world cannot be seen or even touched; they must be felt with the heart." Helen Keller

How would our lives change if we believed that they were sacred? We would treat ourselves as temples. We would feed and rest our bodies properly. We would avoid the people who would desecrate them through abuse or by creating unbearable circumstances in our lives. The care of our sacred temples would be the highest priority in our lives. We would not waste time because we would know the preciousness of our lives.

After we constructed a life plan for treating our bodies as temples, we would reach out to other people, knowing how sacred their lives were. Entering into a relationship of sacredness would mean that we would see the beauty in other people. We would honor their divinity. We would compliment and trust them. We would help them believe in themselves, to find themselves. We would forgive them. We would relinquish all need to be right. We would never blame them for anything. We would know that the purpose of our time together was to experience peace. The light shining on this scene of eternal peace would guide all of our actions. If we saw life as sacred, we would love ourselves unconditionally. We would forgive and forget. We would see everything in life as an adventure, and we would absolutely know that there was no such thing as failure.

You may think these are lofty goals, but you were born with these abilities. When you were an infant, you loved unconditionally. If your parents said or did something to you that was mean-spirited and later apologized for it, you instantly forgave them and forgot all about it.

When you were a little kid, everything you did was an adventure. You played with pots and pans in the kitchen, you played with boxes in the back yard, and you watched ants crawl on your finger. You also had no concept of failure. You were fearless and tried everything. You were born with the sacredness of life. It's only as adults that we get lost, confused and frustrated and allow our egos to take over.

In trying to embrace the sacredness of life, turn to Spirit to give you that sense of peace. Trust in Spirit and look to cultivate your relationship with it.

Exercise:

Name one thing you can do to help you understand how sacred life is.

Affirmation:

All life is sacred, and I consciously acknowledge the sacredness of life in myself and every human being. I promise to treat all life as sacred.

Appendix

Affirmations from A Rose Garden: Living in Concert with Spirit

Part 1: Facts About How Life Works

My life is filled with bouquets of gorgeous roses in full-bloom.

Everything that happens to me—past, present and future—is gently planned by one whose only purpose is my good[1].

I live my life on purpose.

I am the creator of my life!

I embrace my spiritual being.

I live in a world overflowing with abundance. Everything I have, I share with everyone who touches my life.

I am grateful for the gifts that have been given to me, and I share these gifts with everyone with whom I come in contact.

I embrace my life as a physical experience with God on earth. I allow every other human being to live his or her life as a physical expression of God.

I surrender to the divine plan for my life. Everything that happens in my life is for my highest good.

All of my power is in the present moment.

Life is incredibly beautiful. I live for the expression and the experience of the magnificence of life. And everywhere I go and everyone I meet, I search for their magnificence and their beauty. I always find what I am looking for.

I am a winner.

I live only in the present moment and enjoy every moment of my life.

Part 2: Attitudes That Will Minimize Life's Struggles

I am thrilled to have Spirit as my partner to give to me the true perception of the events in my life.

I embrace opposing points of view as my greatest teacher in my growth and development as a student of life on planet Earth.

I constantly express my gratitude for everyone and everything in my life.

I claim my spiritual power to create everything I want in my life by accepting responsibility for it, and I commit to create a life that is exactly what I want it to be.

My life is committed to doing the things that are important to me.

I am grateful for all the gifts that have been bestowed upon me by my creator. I promise to use all these gifts to their fullest ability.

I savor every step in my life.

I'm thrilled that God is my partner, and I trust that all the events that happen to me are gifts from Him. With His assistance, I will find the gift in every event in my life and will be grateful for it.

I know the lessons that disease is there to teach me, and I am committed to learning the lessons without disease.

I am committed to a life of happiness. I release the need to be right.

I am mentally, spiritually and physically flexible and embrace my flexibility as a sign of my openness to receive God's life's love into my life.

I commit to taking the action necessary to develop the skills and talents that I now consider to be vital to a happy and successful life.

My life is a living testament to my being a divine being in a physical body. I invite the divine presence of my creator to work in and through me every moment of my life.

Part 3: Core Principles on Which to Build Your Life

I trust in the partnership I have with the universe to create everything that I tell it I want. The universe and I co-create my life.

The most powerful tool to create in my life is my thoughts. I use my thoughts to create a world that is for my highest good and for the highest good of all concerned.

I embrace change as the highest form of love in life.

I commit to changing the actions in my life in order to get the outcomes that will enable me to live my dream life.

I am _____ (Fill in the blank with whatever you desire for your life.)

I live in a world overflowing with abundance. Everything I have I share with everyone who touches my life.

My divinity is expressed and experienced through the values with which I choose to live my life.

I see and honor the beauty in everyone. I love to explore the differences in everyone I meet. We all have such different and magnificent ways to express our divinity.

As a student of life, I look forward to every communication as a primary source of learning my life lessons.

I am a great listener.

I ride the waves of life's high energy.

Holding onto a grudge is impossible for me, because I see God in everyone.

I choose to express and experience my divine birthright of an inner happiness from God.

Part 4: Points of View to Help You Successfully Navigate Through Life

I am a magnet that attracts great people to teach me life lessons! I am grateful to these teachers. They are here to help me find my way back to my creator.

I use my skills to easily learn my life lessons.

I am grateful for the lessons that are presented to me. I embrace these lessons as gifts of wisdom, knowledge and experience that make me richer, fuller, more complete and more of a divine being.

Life is my teacher, and my most profound lessons come disguised as tragedies.

I love the opportunity for other people show me what I haven't perfected in my life yet.

I use all of my gifts and talents to be all that I can be.

My messages to others are simple and kind.

There is beauty in every person, every event, and I see it everywhere I go!

I am an eager student of life. I am excited about learning my lessons. I completely trust my teacher.

I love and accept myself just the way I am, and I love and accept everyone else just the way they are.

I love observing life.

I turn within to my divine connection to receive the answers to all my questions.

God is the source of my power. He lies within me, and I know that all of my power lies within me, that all wisdom and all answers are within me. I willingly retreat within myself for the answers to all the questions in my life.

Part 5: Beliefs That Will Enable You to Experience Life Fully

I always love myself! I am love.

I give up all hope for a better past. I forgive everyone (including myself) who has hurt me.

I am making a positive difference in the world.

By being true to myself, I set myself free.

I am the person of my dreams. Everything happens for my highest good. I trust in the process of the universe.

Whenever someone does something that could hurt my feelings, I will send him love.

I deserve the very best of all that life has to offer.

Every time I get stuck, I will ask myself, "How else can I look at this?"

I have complete faith in myself, in God and in everyone else in my life.

I am grateful for the gifts that have been given to me, and I share these gifts with everyone with whom I come in contact.

I cherish the wisdom that is available to me from every human and divine being that has ever existed. I ask them to share their wisdom with me, and I thank them for their gift of wisdom. I share my wisdom with whoever wishes to receive it.

I love life, and I live my life fully and without regard for other people's opinions.

I live my life with the intensity that I would live it with the knowledge that this was the last year of my life.

Part 6: Spiritual Beliefs That Will Create More Powerful and Meaningful Relationships

I look for and find God in everyone I meet. The beauty of God shines everywhere.

I am always surrounded by loving beings and loving light, and I am always safe.

I love my body. It is the sacred temple I have chosen to get me through this life.

I love myself.

I pray every single day of my life.

I have an infinite amount of love to give away and don't have much time to give it away.

I experience the ecstasy of letting go and letting God.

Thank you, God, for teaching me to trust you.

I trust God, and I release my need to understand the purpose of the events in my life.

I always ask powerful questions,

I trust that everything that happens in my life is for my highest good. I am always looking for the lesson from every event.

I thank God for teaching me how to get in touch with Him and all the higher beings that reside within me.

All life is sacred, and I consciously acknowledge the sacredness of life in myself and every human being. I promise to treat all life as sacred.

(Footnotes)
[1] Inspired by *A Course in Miracles*, Workbook, p. 247, 255 2nd edition.

About the Author

Jim received his BA from Loras College in Dubuque, Iowa, and his MBA from Loyola University of Chicago. He worked for many years in hospital administration and sales. For the last 14 years he has been a full-time inspirational speaker. He has spoken on the topic of change hundreds of times. The research he has done on personal change and his intense desire to deepen his relationship with God has driven him to create this simple-to-use book, designed to entice you to explore one area of your life that isn't working the way you want. Jim is also a Life Skills Coach. For more information about Jim's seminars and to contact him to set up a coaching relationship with him, visit his web site at www.jimbrownspeaker.com or call him in the Los Angeles area at 800-995-1426.

You may purchase this and other titles directly from Awaken Publishing and receive free shipping in the United States.

Use this order form or go to our website and order online.
http://www.awakenpublishing.net.

Online you may use your credit card.

Mail in this order form and a check to:
(We do not accept credit cards on mail orders)
Checks must be drawn on US banks.

Awaken Publishing
PO Box 25648
Seattle, WA 98165
206-729-3872

Featured titles

A Rose Garden: Living in Concert with Spirit
by Jim Brown $13.95* USD   Qty. _____
Jim Brown shares the wisdom of living from spiritual purpose.

The Mechanics of Consciousness: And Four Ways to Wholeness
by Boston Carter $15.95* USD   Qty. _____
Shaman Boston Carter has developed a theory that explains how each person incarnates choosing one of four possible patterns of perception. There are only four patterns and one of them belongs to you.

If you would like to receive free information on: Other books, speaking seminars and consultation availability, please provide your mailing address below.

Name:_____

Address:_____

City:_____ State:____ Zip:_____

(Footnotes)
* Washington State residents add 8.9% sales tax.